To Mark
Be Proud, Be
Be You.
Sallie
xxx

The Beat Goes On

Supporting you with the practical and emotional side of life when living with heart disease when you're first diagnosed.

SALLIE CRAWLEY

ISBN: 978-1-7399806-3-4

Dedication

I dedicate this book to my father, my best friend and mentor, who I miss with all my heart, Colin Wilson.

He was always there for me, no matter what. He really knew how to listen. He always had some advice or a suggestion that would make me think a little differently.

Whilst my dad lived in today, he always had his eyes on tomorrow. He loved to find the new idea, a different way, a solution to whatever came in his or anyone else's way.

He was always creative, supportive and forward-thinking. I loved him for his ability for being happy for tomorrow believing it would always be better.

There is always a way!

Acknowledgments

I would like to acknowledge the following people for their part in the creation of this book.

Martin Howe for his patience, support and understanding that once I start something, I just don't want to stop. Tanya Kenny for her belief in me and her support in my Facebook community.

Aaron David and Tony Richens-Smith, they gave me courage and feedback that have helped shape this book. I would also like to say thank you to Damien Thorpe and Rob Fearn for their constructive reviews.

Contents

"Anxiety is caused by a lack of control, organisation, preparation, and action."

David Kekich

Disclaimer

The information contained within this book is for general information purpose only. It is not official health advice and is not intended to be used as such.

Any action you take upon the information you find in this book is strictly at your own risk.

Any material or information in this book is not medical or therapeutic and is not intended to diagnose, treat, cure or prevent any medical condition or disease.

If you have any questions pertaining to specific health concerns or you think you may be suffering from a medical condition, you should consult a medical professional immediately.

You should also consult a medical professional before making any changes to your normal lifestyle habits.

Limitation of Warranties

The medical information in this book is provided 'as is' without any representations or warranties, express or implied. This book makes no representations or warranties in relation to the medical information contained within it.

Professional Assistance
You must not rely on the information in this book as an alternative to medical advice from your doctor or other professional healthcare provider.

If you have concerns about any medical matter, your physical or mental health, you should consult your doctor or other professional healthcare provider immediately.

Information included in this book is not intended to replace conventional medicine, it is complementary.

If you think you may be suffering from any medical condition you should seek immediate medical attention.

You should never delay seeking medical advice, disregard medical advice, or discontinue medical treatment because of the information in this book.

Results may vary from person to person. The content of these pages has been developed to assist you and give no guarantee; you yourself can be the only person that can provide a guarantee for your own success.

Liability
Nothing in this medical disclaimer will limit any of our liabilities in any way that is not permitted under applicable law, or exclude any of our liabilities that may not be excluded under applicable law.

By using the information in this book, you hereby consent to my disclaimer and agree to its terms.

Introduction

Inspiring you to survive and thrive emotionally after a cardiac event or when living with heart disease! If in any doubt always check it out and seek medical advice asap.

This book is written from my heart to your heart. I have created it for you because I want you to know you can live your life happy despite having a heart condition.

Having experienced a heart attack in March 2016, I was overwhelmed by how many factors that seemed out of my control were involved in my recovery. I had excellent information from the UK's NHS, I can't fault what I was given and the treatment that I received. But I still felt confused and disorganised. I knew 'the what' I was supposed to change and 'the why' I needed to make the changes.

But I wasn't given 'the how' to make the changes or understand what was going on. This is what I am going to provide for you within these pages.

In the beginning

At the time of my discharge, the most challenging things for me after coming home from Royal Papworth Hospital was the shock, fear, confusion and depression. I no longer trusted myself or my body. I found it hard to remember all that I had been told and I wanted to find answers to questions I didn't know I had.

Why I wrote this book

I want to provide you with the necessary information, the tools and top tips that will help you accept where you are and be able to help yourself feel more confident, in control and less anxious. This accompanies all that you have been told by your medical teams, it is to help you to be able to communicate clearly and understand more about your health and wellbeing.

Whilst I had a heart attack, you may have had a cardiac arrest, open-heart surgery, a transplant or be living with a different heart condition. Whilst our physical experiences will be different, there is a good chance that we will all feel similar emotions and think similar thoughts.

Your frame of mind is the catalyst for your actions. Your thoughts, beliefs and feelings can get in the way of your emotional recovery. Importantly, your mindset is also what underpins your physical and practical lifestyle changes that are the foundations for reducing your risk factors.

The four stages of recovery

How long does it take to recover after a heart disease diagnosis?

That's not an easy one to answer as it can be very different person to person, it also depends on what your diagnosis is. I would say it took me a full 12 months to feel like I was back in the driving seat of life again although my heart attack was more complicated due to other health issues I was experiencing.

I believe living life happy is a journey, not a destination. I like to take the time to enjoy the view, revel at the distances I travel and experience all that is life around me. I'm still learning to love life.

There are four stages of healing and recovery

It's not a straight line like a motorway. It can have some bends along the way, I liken it to being more like a B road with some twists and turns along with ups and downs.

1. the actual heart event/diagnosis/treatment itself.
2. after hospital discharge and before cardiac rehabilitation.
3. during and after cardio rehab going back to everyday life.
4. getting to your 1st 'heartiversary' and the rest of your life.

Your event

I felt fully supported and I trusted my medical team while I was in the hospital and during my treatment. I felt safe, secure and somewhat in control. I had no choice but to give myself mind and body over to the experts and specialists. I also seemed to have a sense of humour, gallows humour, when I am nervous, I try to be funny. I was given lots of advice that all seemed to make sense, shed loads of medication that I didn't have to think about it just arrived and I was fed and watered.

After discharge

Initially, as I was discharged from the hospital, I felt elated. I thought that a few days rest and I would be back on 2 feet (well no not literally as I was in a non-weight bearing leg cast). I believed it was job done and I would be getting on with life. That was not the case though and within hours of being back at home, I crumpled.

I was weak and breathless, the basic crawling up the stairs wasn't possible. I could only get so far then needed a rest. I felt fearful and had panic attacks, I was terrified I would have another event and again I wouldn't notice.

The physical feelings, the fatigue and yet sleeplessness was awful. I even seemed to have difficulty with words, brain fog. I would think something and yet a different word came out of my mouth. I felt anxious, irritable and cross with myself, my life and the situation. I cried for no reason sometimes for a whole day.

Often a cardiac event or intervention is a very traumatic experience by itself. If you had to be resuscitated or experienced additional injuries and surgeries, even more so. At some point after your diagnosis, you have to deal with your own mortality. An idea so traumatic that your brain may withhold it from you consciously to reduce the shock to your system. These emotions do have to be dealt with at some point though.

During cardiac rehab

Once again, I felt supported by the medical team which helped as I could ask questions and exercise in a supported and safe environment. I found that my trust in my physical health increased and my ability and stamina improved.

It was at this point that I gained full insight into the number of practical changes that needed to take place. I needed to understand my risk factors and how to mitigate them. I learnt a lot from the rehab team at my sessions but again they came to an end and I was discharged although I could contact them at any time.

Yet I still found life very confusing, trying to get back to 'normal' and make changes to my lifestyle. When I am at home, how much exercise could I, should I do? How many tablets did I need to take, when and how was I going to remember to take them?

Then I had to learn about the changes to my diet and cholesterol, my blood pressure and at the same time trying to reduce my stress levels. And I was dealing with that brain fog.

I was really struggling; I was so confused by all the change. Life was an emotional roller coaster for me. It was all change; it was all new and it was all confusing.

Getting to 12 months later

This is really a story for another time although this book will help you no matter where you are on your timeline back to living life happy. It's never too late to try different things especially if they help you to feel better.

I will remind you though that it's quite normal to have days when you don't feel so good from time to time. It's how you manage those days and your thoughts that really make a difference. I am still on this journey as I am human and I am a work in progress. As you are too, you can learn the art of living life happy after a cardiac event.

A bit of self-helpy-ness

This is a self-help interactive book; you can help yourself to any or all of the advice and templates I am sharing with you. This is a practical book with ideas that you can use to help you gain **acceptance**, **confidence** and **direction** about the practical activities that need to be addressed in the early stages of cardiac health recovery.

The above are three of six mindset needs that I identified were part of my emotional recovery that were the foundations for my physical recovery. Our thoughts about circumstances impact our thoughts that in turn create our feelings and emotions. Working with them in a practical way underpins your ability to make the life changes we need to make to live a happy and healthy life, effortlessly and easily.

The mindset needs that I base my work of emotional cardiac rehabilitation on are Acceptance, Energy, Hope, Purpose, Confidence and Direction/Action. They helped me evolve into my new life and heal physically, mentally and emotionally. Once I had my foundation built, I found that I needed a different amount of each at different times to help me make the life changes I needed and to learn to love the life I live.

The mindset needs of cardiac recovery in a nutshell

To gain acceptance, energy, hope and confidence you will want to set firm and strong foundations. Here's a simplified version of how meeting these mindset needs can help you to create shifts in your emotional wellbeing and assist you:

1. To **accept** the situation, yourself, what was your life then and what your life is now, along with your limitations. You will know that different is good, if not better - you have your new life, right here, right now.

2. To gain **energy** to fuel your 'new life'. To be inspired to make the necessary changes, to be resilient and to take responsibility for your health and recovery. This is your physical, mental and emotional well-being.

3. To create **hope** for the future, to look forward and find ways of focusing on what you want. Become aware of what you can do/have/want/be so you can love the life you live. Come to terms with your own mortality and look forward to the future and being your best you.

4. To find your **purpose**, your meaning, the getup and go that has you jumping out of bed in the morning. Your 'thing' that makes you feel real and good. Feel motivated to live life, reduce your risks and be happy.

5. To grow your **confidence** to take baby steps (at first), then leap right outside of your comfort zone. To get out of your own way, to overcome fear. You can rid yourself of doubt. You can grow your self-belief.

6. To know your path, the **direction and the action** you want to take. How you are going to work with your medical team towards managing your heart health. Your overall goals, where to start, the steps to take, what is needed to achieve it

and the support that you will need.

The information in this book will help you to make the best choices, learn about medicines, understand the terminology and acronyms used at your appointments and be able to have useful and informative conversations with your medical team. You will find journals, lists and notes sections for you to use.

There are ideas, tips and tricks and techniques that will help you to be purposeful in your communications and determined in your direction to live life with a smile on your face.

Also discussed is the emotional fallout. The rollercoaster ride of thoughts and feelings. You'll also find information to help your nearest and dearest too. They are often forgotten but their world can be as turned upside-down as your own. There are stories from other people that have lived through similar experiences. They share what happened, how they felt and what got them through.

You'll find tips about how to improve your sleep, reduce anxiety, manage pain and prepare to quit smoking too. All of these will empower you to feel good, to be knowledgeable, to feel purposeful, hopeful and energised.

There are so many other medical, physical, emotional and lifestyle factors that contribute to being able to thrive after a heart health diagnosis. I believe that they should be considered holistically.

To get the best results from this book
Read it. There are a lot of people (and I know you are not one of them) that have great intentions but never actually follow through. This book is for reading, not leaving on the table or putting it on the shelf. My words will sit silent and you won't gain the benefits and nothing will change.

Go do it. I have included some activities for you to use. The thing about personal development is that you have to actually do something different. If you always do what you've always done, you'll always get what you've always got. Make sure you give each idea and activity a try. Knowing is not enough! When learning to drive you can learn the rules of the road, you can watch, read and pretend you know how to drive a car but you have to actually get behind the wheel to be able to really drive and travel in the right direction.

It's all about you. Own your thoughts, feelings and actions, they are your responsibility. I can't make the change in your thoughts, feelings and outcomes and nor can anyone else. Trust yourself, you can do this.

Don't expect miracles, it takes your body and mind a while to recover. Be kind to yourself. I don't believe I have all the answers but I do believe that the mind-body connection is a thing!

Be patient, be honest and be gentle with yourself. Living life has never been fair or easy, remember it's the journey, stop occasionally to enjoy the views. Review how far you've come and congratulate yourself for even the smallest achievement or change. They all count towards the art of living happy.

Do what works and drop what doesn't. I am on a mission in life to reassure everyone it is not one size fits all. We are all unique, not one person has the identical fingers print as you so why would the same information, technique or process work for everyone.

I share with you, information, ideas and activities for you to try out, just have a go – some maybe not so good and yet others may be life improving. Think of it as a pick and mix, choose only those that you like. You may find you want to come back to some at a later date.

Your action downloads

Throughout this book, you will find examples of the free resources to help you manage your cardiac and emotional health at home. These include audio relaxation, journals, notes pages and charts. The URL links are included at the end of this book in a chapter of their own.

I do try hard to make life simple and be down with the kids, so where there is a download or URL, I have also included a QR code. You are then able to scan this on your phone and it will take you directly to the links so you have the choice of how to access them.

As I mentioned not everything will work for everybody; unless you give it a go, you won't know what works. Go do it and take action.

The printable downloads are free and you can use them as many times as you wish. If you have any problems, please email me at sallie@myheartandmind.co.uk.

"I am not what you see. I am what time and effort and interaction slowly unveil."

Richelle E Goodrich

Survivors & Thrivers

In the beginning, I felt okay about having a heart attack although it didn't seem real or that serious at first. After a few days, the enormity began to set it as I had more time to think about what happened. I started to feel alone, I had questions but no one to ask and no one to talk to that knew how I felt. Most importantly there was no one to tell me it was going to be alright.

This chapter is a collection of stories from survivors and thrivers. It is their own words describing their event and the heart journey. My hope is that you will take comfort from their words. That you will feel inspired and believe that you can do this because if they did then you sure as hell can too.

Aaron David

My father-in-law had just died and the night before the funeral I'd just finished ironing all of our clothes for the following morning. Getting ready to go to bed I felt a pain in the middle of my chest as if someone was kneeling on my Sternum. I'd had the pain a couple of times over the previous fortnight and it had eventually passed. This time it grew more intense. It wasn't really all that painful; somewhere between discomfort and pain. Then I started shaking and sweating. I insisted it was not worth calling a doctor, especially since we had the funeral the following morning. When my face turned grey, my wife had other thoughts. A paramedic duly arrived and performed an ECG in the bedroom.

"Hmmm. Let's get him downstairs." He said, then. "Ambulance; code red." Into his radio.

Downstairs he performed another ECG and said "You're having a heart attack."

"Having?"

"Yes."

"Not had?"

"No."

The ambulance arrived and a paramedic trundled me quickly and bouncily into the awaiting ambulance.

"If I scream, do we go faster?"

"No."

My eldest son travelled with me, my wife and two other kids followed in her car. We were put into a waiting room and the paramedics stayed with us. Around two hours after the initial call I asked the first paramedic.

"Am I still having a heart attack?"

"Oh yes, it can go on for hours. As long as the muscle is treated before it dies, you'll be OK"

Eventually I was wheeled on a trolley into the catheter lab. A huge TV screen on my left and an operative on my right, behind a clear plastic sheet (X-ray guard). A grey rectangular object hung above my face and chest, approximately the size and shape of a 17″ computer monitor. It whizzed around at the operative's command. I was ordered to keep my right hand still, facing upright. He injected some dye into it and the X-ray thing whizzed around, tracking the dye into my heart. He apologised before injecting something into my wrist; it was VERY cold. Then I could feel him pushing a minute, plastic tube into my wrist. I couldn't feel it as it travelled up the vein inside my arm, across my chest and into the lower rear artery of my heart. My heart began to burn at this point. When a muscle burns it means it's dying. I mentioned this to the doctor and he replied "Keep still." That was when I had the realisation; the realisation that I might not see tomorrow.

In a situation like that your mind goes into overdrive, it processes information at an astonishing rate. I accepted my death; I wasn't happy about it but I accepted it. There's no appeals process; how you feel about it is irrelevant, not wanting to die doesn't make it any less likely to happen. There is no grim reaper, no big baddie to come and carry you away. Your DNA has an expiry date written into it and my time was now; I was weirdly OK with it. My Mum had died when I was twenty and although I was devastated, I'd turned out well enough. The mortgage was covered by insurance and my life assurance would pay out £100,000. I relaxed and waited for the inevitable. The thing I found most upsetting was that the last face I would see was a very pleasant, young, Indian doctor. Not my wife, not my children, not my siblings or my best friend, a young doctor. I didn't even know his name. A few minutes later...

"Got it!"

Within two seconds the pain vanished. The X-ray machine swung out of the way, he swept the plastic sheet away and smiled at me.

Then he gave me a stern look as he stood up.

"You nearly died tonight because you smoke."

"Not anymore." I smiled back.

My wife and kids raced home and caught an hour's sleep before they attended the funeral. I of course couldn't attend.

I was kept in Wythenshawe Hospital for two more days, just in case I had a relapse or a bad reaction to the drugs, which I will have to take for the rest of my life.

I'm sure most of us have a mental image of what a heart attack is like; the agonised expression on the face, fingers claw at ribs, collapse on floor, writhe around, die. That's probably what a cardiac arrest is like but most of us get a heart attack first. What I found most shocking was how painful it wasn't. The paramedics asked me repeatedly how painful it was on a scale of one to ten. My answers bobbled between four and seven. It just didn't feel painful enough to be fatal.

Had my wife and daughter not been home I would probably be dead. Fellas; don't risk the wait.

If you feel a pressing pain on your chest, GET TO A & E!

I've criticised the NHS as much as anyone but I owe them my life. Thank you, NHS.

So, the epilogue.

I'd love to tell you my life is better than it was before, that it was cathartic and I'm a better man than I was since having a heart attack. It isn't and I'm not. The only positive thing is I'm alive and I shouldn't be. I can tell you it's not as bad as I imagined it was going to be. I can still work; I'm not disabled in any way; I'm just not as able as I was before. I was fifty years old when it happened and was pretty sure I wouldn't make fifty-one. When I did, I didn't think I'd make fifty-two. Then I didn't think I'd make fifty-five. Approaching my fifty-sixth birthday I don't expect to make sixty. At sixty I won't expect to make seventy. We've all been through a traumatic experience.

We've all been closer to death than we're comfortable with. It isn't a death sentence, life goes on. Live It.

Julie Wren

The first time I learnt that I have a bicuspid aortic valve was when my doctor referred me to a cardiologist because he could hear a murmur in my heart during a routine check-up. I was in my 20s. The cardiologist explained the cause of the murmur, as well as my prognosis. It made sense to me then, why it was throughout my childhood and adolescence that despite participating in a lot of physical activities, like sports and dance, I was never quite able to reach the same levels of fitness as others.

I returned to the cardiologist for check-ups every three years until my mid-40s, when these became annual. This is when an aneurysm on my aorta was identified and monitored for size and growth. I was prescribed a statin and blood-pressure-lowering medications. I have always cared about my health. My mother, a brilliant cook, instilled in me the Mediterranean-type of diet, long before it was researched and even had a name. Eating healthily is normal for me.

I enjoy activity. For instance, I 'twalk' (simultaneously walk and talk with friends) at least 10,000 steps each day, and I attend aqua aerobics regularly. Hence, my heart, aside from the structural issues associated with bicuspid aortic valve, is healthy in every other way.

By my early 50's, the onset of symptoms began, mostly to do with heart palpitations, and later, with an occasional sense that I did not have enough oxygen in my body. My physical activities gradually lessened, and I began modifying my lifestyle to accommodate for this. This process was so subtle, that it was almost unnoticeable. But I found that I began avoiding flights of stairs or hills. Instead of walking along with others, I often arrived at venues early, so that I could walk there at my own pace.

This was not to hide my condition, but so as not to inconvenience others. I also found it was an avoidance strategy. Some well-intentioned people who knew nothing about my condition became overtly protective. They tried to help by giving me advice about how to care for myself based on something they had read or heard or someone they knew who had similar, but not quite the same, heart issues as me.

In my late 50s, I was offered my dream job overseas (PNG). Assured that I could get home very quickly (comprehensive insurance that included expatriation to Australia for medical care) and in consultation with my cardiologist about how best to manage my condition and symptoms, I took that job. My husband and I packed up our home, placed our belongings into storage and leased our home for a year. We were going on an adventure of a lifetime!

Unfortunately, with Covid-19, I was only in my job for six months when we had to return to Australia. With no direct flight to Perth, where we were from, we stopped in Brisbane and were required to self-isolate for two weeks. To our surprise, our home state of Western Australia shut its borders during this time, and we were unable to return. Stranded in Brisbane, we leased a small place and enjoyed the next few months.

However, my symptoms suddenly worsened. I started to wheeze and could hardly walk through being so breathless. My husband took me to the emergency department. The doctors checked my heart and lungs and concluded that either I was anxious/stressed, or I had asthma. I argued that it was neither of these: that it was in fact my heart function. I could feel it. I had very odd sensations where different parts of my heart seemed to be triggering at different times like it lacked synchronicity. The wheezing was associated with the new symptoms and not my lungs. However, I was prescribed asthma medications, which I took. After a few weeks, my condition somewhat worsened. All my symptoms became more prominent than before.

After a 35-year patient-doctor relationship with my general practitioner in Perth, I found myself in search of a new doctor in Brisbane. To my delight, I found one just as caring and knowledgeable. He not only dismissed the prognosis that I had either anxiety or asthma, but by listening to my heart, he was able to very accurately described to me what I was sensing (regurgitation) and the reasons why (some quantity of oxygenated blood flowing backwards). I asked many questions and he answered me so that I could understand. He referred me to a cardiologist.

My new cardiologist in Brisbane compared my current heart results to those I had in Perth the year before. He concluded two things: firstly, the echocardiogram and MRI results indicated that my valve function and the size of my aneurysm had only fractionally worsened from the previous year, and secondly, given that I had suddenly become so symptomatic, he was sufficiently alarmed and suggested surgery. He explained that symptoms and quantitative results from MRIs and echocardiograms etc do not always concur. He elaborated that sometimes, some patients who are very ill according to these tests, exhibit no symptoms at all, and vice versa, as was my case. I appreciate that he was not dismissive and took seriously what I had described was going on. He referred me to a thoracic surgeon.

The surgeon explained the procedure to me with diagrams and also answered many of my questions. We decided on the best day for my surgery and chose the hospital I would go to.

The first thing I recall after surgery is that I could breathe with ease and each breath seemed unbelievably clear and crisp. The thoracic surgeon asked me how I was feeling, and my response was, 'Wow, is this what it's like to breathe?', to which he smiled and said I was doing really well.

From there, my recovery journey was gradual, two steps forward, one step back. I had to return to ICU after a week in my hospital bed because my blood pressure suddenly and inexplicably plummeted, and the recovery team needed to resuscitate me. This was a solitary glitch on an otherwise forward-moving recovery journey.

It has been eight months now and I still find that there are days I feel tired and slow. I hypothesise that this relates to the anaesthetic procedures more so than to my heart. I just take each day as it comes. I am generally back to doing everything I enjoy, and I am as physically, cognitively and socially active as ever. Every now and then, first thing in the morning when I wake up, I catch myself feeling that awe at how easily I can breathe, but these times are fewer and my memory of feeling breathless and wheezy is fading. I feel so grateful that I live in a country where I can have the medical treatments I needed.

I look back now as I write my story and I see that my surgery was something I had to have, to fix a physical problem I was born with. I note that my father and his brother (my uncle) both had bicuspid valves and they think that their father (my grandfather) died from it back in the mid-60s. The next generation of the family have been tested and my niece has been found to also have a bicuspid valve. She is in her 20s, and her blasé attitude to her heart issues, very much reminds me of me, at that age.

Two take-aways from my experience are:

- Trust my senses: my account of what I feel is going on with my heart is valid and reliable. My medical care is a team effort. The diagnosis and treatment have to be both quantitative (medical test results such as MRIs and echo) and qualitative (my account of how I am feeling at every stage);

- Gratitude: I am grateful that for me, a good diet and ongoing physical, social and mental activities are my life (and not something I consciously have to think about or do). After attending cardiac therapy and meeting others for whom heart surgery was an emergency, I am grateful that my heart issues were not a surprise (or shock), that my heart function now is excellent (as the structural issue has been corrected) and that I am responsible for my own wellbeing (I can do this).

As my open-heart surgery was never an emergency, perhaps that is why I perceive it as nothing more than just an event in my life. It is what it is. I do not dwell on it. I do not reflect on it and wonder why me? It does not stop me from doing what I want to do. For a while, it took centre stage in my life because I was symptomatic, but now, I rarely give it a thought or talk about it (only when I have to have a check-up). I do not fear that my heart will suddenly stop because I trust in my care of it.

There is too much else in life that is way more interesting and that is where my focus is now.

Maria Wilkinson

In August 2020 I awoke from a dream crying with really bad chest pain. In my dream I was dead. I was looking down at my body when all of a sudden, my father who had passed away nearly 3 years earlier appeared. Behind him was a blue sky and white clouds; he looked at me and said 'I love you princess but you have to go back '. All of a sudden, like in movies, I got sucked back into my body, as I entered back, I woke up crying holding my chest. I had suffered really bad acid for years so just put the pain down to bad indigestion and went back to sleep.

Fast-forwards to 21st September 2020. I went into hospital as an outpatient to have a gastroscopy camera down my throat. When they pulled the camera out, I had severe pain in my chest just like the night of my dream. I told them and they did an ECG. They said was normal and my pain was more than likely gas from when they inflated my stomach and it would pass.

Back home my husband told me to go on bed rest so I did. Late teatime my pharmacist rang to see how my new diabetes injections were going. I asked his advice about the pain and explained what had happened that day. He said he would call me back as he wanted to catch one of the doctors from the adjoining surgery before they left. He called me back within 20 minutes. The doctor had said as my ECG was normal, he was concerned about a pulmonary embolism. He wanted me to go straight to accident and emergency and explain what happened and what he said so I did.

They took me straight into a room and hooked me up to all the machines and took various blood samples. After about 2 hours the doctor came back, he explained my ECG again seemed normal. But the blood test they do to test for active heart attack showed my reading, which should be 5, but I was 265. He explained I definitely was having a heart attack and he was admitting me to the cardiac ward which he did, I was there for a week. I had to keep a portable heart monitor on while I was in there. They also ran more blood tests. They did an angiogram and ultrasound of my heart and this showed one of my arteries was 70% blocked.

They decided to transfer me to another hospital. The next day I was taken into surgery to have a stent fitted in my heart. I love anything medical and the surgeon told me to turn my head so I could see the monitor he was viewing while inserting the stent. I was so fascinated watching this thing get fed up my arm and then across my chest into my heart and back out. I think weirdly watching it distracted me from what they were doing as it felt like I was watching a TV show instead of me lol.

Anyway, later the cardiologist came and asked if I had ever had any pain like that before. I laughed and said please don't commit me but I had a dream a month earlier and I told him about it. I honestly thought 'he's going to think I'm nuts' but he said based on all my tests it looked like I'd recently had another heart attack before I was admitted with this one. He said my dream was more than likely a near-death experience and not just a dream.

He put me on a few meds and changed a few that I was already on. He arranged for new insulin injections too as my diabetes was still very high, I was sent home the next day. It honestly took me a good two months to recover but I did have numerous 20+ other health issues too.

Lately, in fact just a few weeks ago, I had the same pain so went to the hospital. Fortunately, I was not having a heart attack. I had scans to rule out things like gallbladder problems liver or kidney problems and they were all clear. The doctor said he would contact my cardiologist as he believed there was something going on with my heart that needs further investigation.

My cardiologist actually called me yesterday, based on the tests and my history he is arranging another appointment for an angiogram as he thinks I may need more stents put in my heart. So now I'm just waiting for the appointment.

What I did realise during my recovery was that it was OK to feel like crap and not be able to do what I wanted because that was my body putting its foot down. It is saying no your heart needs to rest. Fortunately, I had my husband and two sons to help me and I knew I could ask for help. I also found comfort and advice from groups on Facebook from people who had gone through it already. Even teachers from my son's special education school would ring to see how I was and ask if there was any help we needed.

You think having a heart attack is a sad scary lonely thing but I realised just how many cared about me. I also realised that those who I thought were good friends but weren't that good a friend really. Anyway, hopefully, my angiogram will give some answers and a treatment plan so can feel a bit better.

Peter Robinson

My heart journey began way back in 2004. It began with me collapsing on-site in London, building a kid's playground.

Rushed to Bolton Hospital for tests etc. but me being me, left because all the drugs they gave me, made me feel fine. A month later I didn't feel well at all and asked the wife to make me an appointment with the DOCTOR.

That was Tuesday and he would see me Friday morning. Carried on as always, though I was vomiting and feeling very tired. Thursday night, the wife, daughter and her boyfriend went to bingo as usual. I stayed home alone and caught up on some sleep. They got back around 11ish and off we went to bed.

Woke at 2.15 am feeling very short of breath, arm and jaw aching like hell. Told the wife I needed to go to A&E as something wasn't right. Everyone up and as I was the only one not had a drink, drove to A&E with a cigarette in my mouth.

Back then it was just another guy that was filling up the waiting room. Got taken back to a trolley and told to stop complaining as they were very busy. Some 3 hours later and a hospital sister told me if I insisted on complaining then I would have to leave, as they had already given me paracetamol for the pain.

Doc finally arrives and gives me an ECG, all hell breaks loose and I now have enough staff around me to run an entire ward. Into the Resuscitation room and pumped full of drugs and stuff. Heart rate is now in the mid-20s and was rushed into the cardiac ward.

No, I can't have a cup of tea and need to relax.

Next thing it's Sunday afternoon and some bugger has nicked a couple of days off me. I now have more wires and tubes than London underground.

A week later and am free to go, but need to see someone about stents in another hospital. 3 weeks after my enforced long weekend break, it's time for stents.

Getting to Manchester infirmary at 8 am is no easy task and I arrive 9 minutes late. Some lady in dark blue is well miffed and tells me they are waiting for me.

My wife leaves and I am put in a gown and told to wait on the bed.

At 4 pm everyone else has been down and gone home. Me still waiting for the people that were earlier waiting for me.

Having never been to a Cath lab, I was more than a little nervous by now and my sugars were getting very low. I explained that if I was going to have to wait any longer, I need to eat something now or leave.

Just then a porter turns up and takes me to the lab. Lots of questions and explain to them that I am allergic to Iodine and the contrast they use. I'm then rolled into the lab and the very same nurse that did the 20 questions paints me with Iodine. This almost instantly burns my groin area. I now have more confidence in finding an honest MP than this lot of clowns.

Two hours into the procedure I tell them I need a pee, no you don't the guy says, it's the drugs.

30 minutes later I again tell him I need to pee, so stop whatever you're doing so I can go to the loo. It's all in your mind he insists, but we will get a bottle. Three bottles of pee and him puffing away. I tell him that he now has a piece of my mind.

He carries on for another hour and then tells me he has done his best, but I will need to come back for more on another day. The LAD is now 75% clear but the circumflex is completely blocked. What was supposed to be a morning trip is now an overnight stay.

Roll on 3 years and I wake with an elephant sat on my chest. I get the car out and drive to A&E once again and this time they don't even offer me a trolley. Into the resus room and another round of drugs and wires. Then transferred after a week to Manchester Hospital for more stents.

What do you know, it's the same guy as last time and the look on his face was so funny! This time he has another guy with him and they each do a groin each. Several hours later they admit defeat. They agree that it isn't possible to stent the circumflex, but put did stents the full length of the LAD.

Home after a few days looking like Purple Ronny with all the hematomas. A week off work and back to the grindstone (who can live on £62 a week of sick pay).

Roll forward to 2009 and once again I am driving to A&E, something isn't right but I am sure it isn't a heart attack.

Nothing like the others, just feeling exhausted and even breathing is hard work. Instant ECG says otherwise and again am in the cardiac ward. Those injections belly sting like hell, as anyone that has had them, will tell you. I look like someone has used me for target practice.

I can't go to Manchester Hospital as my white blood count is through the roof so I must have an infection. I reminded them that they had given me steroids to avoid the complications of the contrast. The penny drops and they arrange for me to be transferred at 6 am the next day.

Nobody told the ambulance though so they never turned up. A private one arrives at 4.30 pm and off we go again.

OMG, it's the same guy, so I now feel very anxious indeed. He tried twice and failed already. 45 minutes later and he once again fails miserably and I get sent back to Bolton.

DVLA (Driver and Vehicle Licensing Agency) have nicked both my licenses. HGV (Heavy Goods Vehicle) and PSV (Public Service Vehicle) but I can drive the car.

My doctor and cardiologist agree I will never be able to work again, so it's full time sick from now on.
It's 2016 and they decide I should have an angiogram to see if they can do anything else to improve my life. In August I go for an angiogram and they tell me they can fix most of my problems with bypass surgery.

In January 2017 I go in for a big operation. I am scared and alone. I spend the first night trying not to think. I am first to go at 7.45 am and a really nice guy chats with me while he gets me ready to go to the theatre.

I wake up at around 5 pm and am told the op didn't work as they couldn't find suitable graft sites. I now have a free zipper down my chest and my right leg, but no bypass. I was hidden away in a single room, so it doesn't upset those waiting to go down. I am

left to think the worst and nobody to talk to about it at all.
I was discharged after a week and a letter for cardio rehab arrives. The rehab team tell me I don't qualify because I haven't had a heart attack or a bypass. You're on your own now mate, sink or swim.

I spend many hours every day, searching the internet for anything that may help me, get to grips with it all. A guy pops up and asks if I want to join a new Facebook group for hearties.

Why not I think, can't hurt and it may even help me or others. So, I join his group and there are now 12 of us. We chat and swap stories, how things help and what you can and can't do. The group grew superfast and I am now an admin, keeping tracks and folk in line. We have 6,000 members from all over the globe. I found out how things are different in other countries and how treatment and drugs used are.

I was there for over two years, giving advice finding out things that others had asked about, so I had to research it all. I must admit, I know more about my heart, lungs etc than most doctors.

So many changes of drugs, so many cardiologists, so many different hospitals. Statins, ace inhibitors, beta-blockers. I've had them all at some time or other.

If I help one person a day or make one person smile/grin. Then that's a good day for me. Life has changed, I have changed, but every day I make a promise, to do something to help another cardiac survivor.

My heart and other issues have been life-changing and not for the better at times. I try and stay positive because those days that I feel like crap are just speed bumps on the road. They get left behind, but I know another one will turn up.

I have survived for 17 years and promised I would be there for my grandkids leaving school. 9 years to go, but I will fight for every one of them. I've taken those kids to Turkey, Egypt and Tunisia. South Africa got cancelled (due to covid) but I am going to take them to see the real wildlife one day.

Never give up because you have a setback, never give up because you're having a tough time. Plenty of others in a worse position and if they can smile, so can I.

I don't have good health, but I do have a wonderful family. Who needs to be perfect when they have a perfect family around them?

Life is not about what you have, it's about who you are. Me I am just another guy that looks old and walks very slow. Inside is a guy that is 21 and wants to carry on, until I get the letter from the Queen.

I think of this song as my very own at times, because I will always be there for those who need me. Make sure you have a listen on YouTube folks.
"James Taylor - You've Got a Friend"

Peter's further thoughts:

Having a heart attack or other issues with the heart, isn't the end. It's a whole new chapter in your life. Sure, you miss out on some things, but you gain a brand-new start in a brand-new life. Set simple but achievable targets (not unreachable ones that you will fail to achieve). New hobbies and interests come along and get you wanting to try more stuff. Life has changed, but it is now up to you, to make it your life. Every single one of us is different, so never judge your life, with what others have achieved. You didn't before, so why do it now.

Never be afraid to ask questions, nobody knows all the answers.

Share your achievements and successes and share the things that you struggle with (advice from others could help you hit those targets). Life before was full of "what ifs" and it will always be that way.

Having a heart attack can be life changing, but so can having kids. You are far stronger than you think, hell your still here and alive. You are a survivor, you are a winner, and once more you will smile and say "I got this".

After almost 2 decades I get what it's all about, it's about you living and achieving. It's not a race, it's not about being better or as good as. It's about you and your life. You decide what's best for YOU, not some stranger or other individual. There are no strict rules that apply to everyone.

Rob Fearn

I was just a regular bloke who had just turned 50. I don't smoke and never have. I liked a few beers per week but nothing excessive. According to the crazy figures that weight watchers and doctors work to I was about 2 stones overweight but at 6ft tall I carried it well. My diet was ok. I maybe had a few too many takeaways but ate cereals, rice, fruit etc on a daily basis.

I work as an external salesman, driving throughout the East Midlands calling on several customers per day. On the 18th of June 2019, I went off to work, as usual, feeling fine. I was sat chatting with my first customer of the day when I noticed an email pop saying that my boss wanted to spend the day out with me later that week. Although my boss is the nicest bloke you would ever wish to meet, I instantly started to get anxious. I had only been working for the company for two months so it would be our first day out together. Where should I take him? Should I make prior appointments? What will he think of my sales style? What will he think of me? Just a few of the questions which flooded into my mind.

Within a couple of minutes, I had a slight aching in the right-hand side of my chest. Nothing too bad (in fact I have had far worse indigestion). I was comforted in the fact that the pain was on the right and I felt sure that your heart is on the left. I carried on my day without paying too much attention to the pain and concentrating more on my pending day out with my boss.

By early afternoon the pain had extended into my right bicep. It still wasn't too bad so I assumed it must have been a pulled muscle. In fact, when I arrived in a customer's car park, he had a skip for rubbish and when I got out of the car, I did a few standing press-ups on the side of the skip to stretch out the muscle. (Turns out this is not recommended when having a heart event).

Anyhow, I went in to see the customer, then when I returned to the car I started pouring with sweat. My clothes, hair, everything was dripping with sweat. I called my wife and asked her what she thought. She tried to reassure me and said that it was probably just a panic attack. I checked on my phone and the nearest cottage hospital was only 1 mile away so I thought I would pop in to check things out.

I drove to the hospital (again not recommended) and walked up to the small A&E reception. A sign said two hours wait so I turned around and started walking back to the car. Thankfully the pain increased so I turned around again. I walked into reception clutching my chest and dripping with sweat and thankfully they recognised the signs and rushed me straight in. They started doing ECGs and blood tests etc.

At this point, I was still thinking it was bad indigestion until I said to one of the nurses that I hadn't had time to put a parking ticket on my car. He turned to me and said in a serious tone that that was the very least of my problems. It was getting serious. They had called for an emergency ambulance to blue light me to the cardiac unit at the City Hospital at Nottingham. I was wheeled out to the ambulance with the pads already on my chest in case I went into full cardiac arrest. Strangely all I was thinking about at the time was that I was glad that they wheeled me out through the A&E department so all the people in the waiting room could see that I wasn't faking it when I jumped the queue.

On arrival at the City Hospital, I was taken straight into the Cath lab. Naively I thought that anything as serious as messing around with someone's heart would be done under general anaesthetic but that is not the case.

They went in through my wrist and found that I had a 100% blockage in the LAD. It turns out that is pretty high on the serious intervention required scale.

They inserted a stent to open up the LAD and the relief was almost instant.

I was then wheeled into the critical care cardiac ward. After settling in the surgeon came to see me and said all had gone well and that I was lucky that I had gone to the hospital when I did. Now that the real emergency was over, he had had the chance to have a look at the imagery properly and thought that I may have had another narrowing that would need looking at. It was hard to tell as all the veins and arteries go into a spasm during a heart attack so it may be ok but while I was there, they may as well go back in a few days later to have another look.

I then had a few days wired up to monitors which I found really reassuring plus the nursing staff were also superb. I had a chat with the cardiac rehabilitation coordinator (I'm sure she probably had a better title than that) and she asked all about my history.

Do I smoke, drink, diet, exercise etc. All the answers were ok although I should imagine that like 90% of the population, we could all do a little better. When she asked about stress I broke down. I didn't think I had a problem but it all came flooding out. I had started a new job, I had an unrelated health condition which affected me daily, my mum was suffering from advanced Alzheimer's and was nearing the end of her life, a credit card balance which wasn't excessively large but still played on my mind etc.

It was agreed that these issues would be picked up by the cardiac rehab team and that I would be referred for help.

Anyhow, I spent another 6 days waiting for my turn in the Cath lab again. The surgeon came and explained that they would go in through my wrist again and put a pressure wire through the narrowing to check the flow rate to see if I needed a second stent.

I was more scared this time as it wasn't an emergency so I had more time to worry about it. I also had an unexplainable feeling of doom. My wife had been supporting me all the way through and had been back and forward to the hospital while looking after the house and our pets. On this particular morning, I had texted her to stay at home and come to see me in the afternoon after the procedure.

I also had encouraging and supportive text messages from a friend who I played pool with. He really stepped up to the plate when I needed it most. On the flip side, some people who I expected to be there appeared to distance themselves. Maybe they didn't know what to say but they could have tried.

Anyhow, my turn came and I went into the Cath lab. They said that once they introduced the dye into my system that my chest would feel tight but it would only last for a minute then it would ease rapidly. The pain started and I can remember it being really bad. The pain went from my chest to my arms, neck, right up to my ears. I started counting thinking that once I get to 60 that I would be through the worst of it.

I got to around 12 and then nothing.

The next that I knew was an horrendous pain in the back of my leg, a nurse holding my hand and saying my name and someone else pressing on my knee saying straighten your leg.

I didn't know who I was, where I was and what was happening.

It turned out that I had a VF arrest and had to be shocked. They believe that it could have been caused by a R on T ectopic. The shock had caused my leg muscle to spasm and cramp up hence the reason my leg was in agony and someone was trying to straighten it.

I was monitored for a further 24 hours then discharged.

My wife was delighted to have me home and I obviously felt the same about being with her but the thought of leaving the hospital petrified me. Other patients in the hospital were desperate to get out and go home but, in a way, I was the opposite. I loved the reassurance of the monitoring and the nurses on hand if anything went wrong.

So, after leaving the hospital I signed up for the cardiac rehabilitation program. I cannot believe that anyone would refuse this offer. It is superb.

I initially got to meet a nutritionist and expected to be lectured on eating lettuce leaves for every meal for the rest of my life. It wasn't like that at all. It was more about making improvements and moderating. Common sense really but still good to be reassured. If you like chocolate there's a lot of evidence that a small amount of dark chocolate does your heart good. Stuffing a family size dairy milk down your neck every day, not so good.

If you like a drink. A glass of red wine from time to time again does your heart good. 12 pints of Stella on a Saturday night, not so good.

If you like a takeaway. treating yourself to a chicken tikka with a vegetable side dish from time to time won't do you any harm. KFC every night, not so good.

It all makes sense really and you actually start to look forward to your 'cheats' even more. Once a month I have fish and chips and look forward to it and enjoy it more than I ever have before. Apart from that, I eat very healthily, eating more fruit and veg than ever.

The second part of the rehab program was the exercise program. Again, it was great to try and push yourself a little with the reassurance that you had a couple of trained cardiac nurses on hand if things went wrong.

Thirdly the exercise program was followed by a mindfulness session. I was sceptical at first but just having a 20-minute lie down after all the exercise was good. I struggled to buy into the story being read out but started to realise that it cleared my head of worries for a short time at least.

So, nine weeks after my initial MI I woke up early one morning with an all too familiar pain in the right-hand side of my chest. We called 111 to get advice and they immediately dispatched an emergency ambulance. My ECG was ok but due to my symptoms and history, they had to take me to the hospital. They did a blood test and found that my troponin level was slightly high at 45 (nothing compared to the original MI when it peaked at 168,420 which I believe could be an Olympic and commonwealth record) I stayed for another 4 hours for a second test where the level had increased to over 80. They decided to keep me in and send me to the Cath Lab the following morning to investigate. It turned out that I did need a 2nd stent after all. Maybe the checks hadn't been completed the first time due to the emergency of the cardiac arrest.

I left the hospital two days later and restarted the rehab program a couple of weeks later.

By this time, I had bought an Apple Watch to monitor my pulse, blood pressure machine, thermometer etc and started to monitor myself obsessively. I showed all the figures to the cardiac nurse at one of my rehab sessions. She advised me not to get too hung up or stressed over the figures as it works similar to white coat syndrome where your figures get worse when you stress over them. She told me to concentrate more on how I felt.

I had a few problems early doors with my new collection of medications but I would advise anyone to report back to your DOCTOR or cardiologist if you have problems. Not every pill will suit every person and there are dozens of alternatives. In the early days at various times, I had palpitations, night sweats, night cramps, vivid nightmares etc. These were all side effects of the medications which could be fixed by switching to an alternative.

As regards my mental health unfortunately this is where the NHS let me down a little. I signed up for 'talking therapy' through my doctors' surgery. I waited 6-8 weeks for an assessment phone call from someone clearly reading from a script asking me questions to finally come to an assumption that I was suffering with anxiety and stress. This would then mean that I could go onto the 12 weeks+ waiting list. She did ask if I had suicidal thoughts which I would hope would have led to faster treatment but thankfully I hadn't.

I paid for counselling privately. Overall, it did me good just to open up to someone who was impartial. We tried lots of things. Hypnosis, tapping, mindfulness, etc.

Most didn't work for me but just talking definitely helped. Being a typical stubborn bloke, I didn't think I would be open up, especially to another man, but I found myself sitting there crying on every single visit.

I also started on a low dose of anti-depressants from my doctor. They took a couple of months to have any effect. I was initially scared that I would end up like a zombie but it's not like that at all. It just helps me to cope.

I would encourage anyone to try all different types of support for mental health. Just like the tablets, everyone is different and what works for one won't work for another.

For example, hypnosis.
I have always been in sales all my working life so am used to smashing targets and achieving the impossible. If someone says to me count to 12 and by the time you get to 8 you will be so relaxed that you can't see the numbers, I will deliberately count to 13 to prove them wrong. I'm stubborn like that so probably not the best candidate for hypnosis.

But don't give up, there's something for everyone.

A great piece of advice that my cardiologist gave me when I was panicking about dying was: I am aware of my condition, I have a team of experts behind me, I am doing my best to live a healthy life, I am on all the right medication so I am far, far, far less lightly to die from a heart attack than the millions of people around the world who have a serious life-threatening heart condition and are totally unaware.

As a side note to all this my wife also ended up needing counselling. All the focus is on the person who is suffering the heart event but it is usually even tougher for the close family. My wife and I have been together since we first started dating at the age of 13 in school. We got married on the 11th anniversary of our first date and have been together since. Neither of us wanted children (we have 8 nephews and nieces if we needed a kid fix) so apart from pets, we are everything to each other. I have had several near-death experiences and although my wife is a rock and as strong as she can be during a health crisis, once the dust settles it all comes down on her like a tonne of bricks.

Tony Richens-Smith

In January 2020, I had finally finished my IT career of 34 years after spending the last 18 months in a very stressful job. The plan was to increase my dog behaviour work, having run my own business (called "Think Dog Positive"), since 2017. Unfortunately, just as I left that secure job, the Covid-19 pandemic became headline news. Great timing! Fortunately, I started working at Booths supermarket (a local family firm), doing 3 shifts a week and continuing my dog behaviour business around them. Considering what was going on in the "outside world", life was going well for us.

Working in the supermarket meant I was probably the healthiest I'd ever been. Sure, I was overweight by about 1.5 stone, but I was a fitter chap than before, and had more energy. I walked to work, I haven't smoked for over 30 years (and wasn't very good at it when I did smoke in my late teens). I only drank one bottle of Ale per week (or two if I was feeling adventurous), we didn't eat lots of takeaways and as far as I know there is no family history of heart disease. The family even managed to avoid catching Covid (a pretty good thing considering 3 of our household are "key workers"). Stress was low, I was enjoying both my jobs and spending a bit more time with my family. I was even part-way through writing a dog behaviour book. Then it happened …

February 5th, 2021 … it was a day like any other. It was Friday and my shift at the supermarket started at 6am. It is a physical job - moving pallets of stock and restocking shelves. There was a fair amount of "stuff" to get out before the store opened to the public. When the "fruit and veg" delivery arrived, we worked in a team of two or three to get it out on display and went for my first break of the day at 9:20am. The deliveries cause me to sweat a fair amount, and I drink lots of cool water on my break. Only this time, I didn't stop sweating! Not wanting to draw attention to myself (and feeling slightly nauseous), I first went to the toilet and then sat outside to cool down. My manager came out and said I looked "really grey".

By this point, I had convinced myself that I had Covid - in my eyes it made perfect sense, I was cold but sweating so obviously this meant I had a fever. My wife came and picked me up and when we got home, I stripped off and fell into bed, trying to warm up. At this point, my right wrist had started to ache, and I felt like I had slight indigestion. She took my temperature, and it was around 35.5 C, which didn't make much sense because of all the sweating. To top it all off, my right arm (between wrist and elbow) was really beginning to annoy me. I remember saying I would happily cut it off if she brought me a knife. It wasn't a sharp pain, more a bad ache which didn't ease by changing position. After speaking with our GP surgery, she called for an ambulance – they mentioned "heart attack" but my symptoms didn't sound right, so we were confused.

The Paramedics were very efficient and after performing an ECG, one of them turned to me and said, "Well Mr Richens-Smith, I can confirm you are having a heart attack". I was given medication and second crew arrived with some Morphine. At one point, I had 4 paramedics, a trainee, my wife, and my young son all stood around me (lying in the bed, almost naked). It was surreal! Once I got downstairs (that's a whole different story), they popped me into the ambulance and told us I was going "straight onto the table" for surgery. Covid restrictions meant she would not be able to come with me, so we hugged each other, and it all suddenly became real. She was led out of the ambulance, the doors slammed shut and I didn't know if I would ever see her again …

I was "blue-lighted" to Blackpool Victoria hospital and had an angiogram, followed by a stent. Later, I was told by the consultant that I had had a 100% blocked LAD (left anterior descending) artery and would have died without the emergency treatment. He also told me I would have to come back in 8 weeks for a further stent to be put into my circumflex artery because that also had a significant blockage. I stayed in hospital for 3 days with no visitors and had to wear a mask for 24 hours a day (apart from eating and drinking) because of Covid restrictions. It was the loneliest time of my life and without becoming good friends with a couple of other chaps, I'm not sure I would have coped. Apart from the emotional trauma of being separated from those I love deeply; I was petrified of dying (not least because I still had a book to finish writing). In one hour, I had gone from being in total control of my life (and being happy), to not knowing what would happen in the next seconds, minutes, days.

When I came out of hospital, everything was delayed because of Covid. At the time of writing, it is June 2021 (almost 5 months after my heart attack) and I have only just started the Cardiac Rehabilitation Programme. I don't know what it was like before, but without those important face-to-face connections with professionals, and with limited communication, my family and I feel like we have been in a state of Limbo for months. I wish I had written down questions as I thought of them because when I did manage to speak to someone, I invariably forgot them.
In April 2021 I went back into Blackpool Victoria for a second angiogram and a wire pressure test. During the pre-admission appointment, I was told I also had a blockage in the left main artery, and they wanted to see if it needed stenting as well as the circumflex artery. This was the first time I had heard this, and I had to go back and tell my wife that I might be having two stents instead of one. On the day of the procedure, they performed the angiogram and the wire pressure test but did not put any stents

in. I was briefly told the left main had sufficient blood flow and they would manage the blockage with medication. The circumflex was not mentioned.

I was sent home the same day but became violently ill due to an adverse reaction with the muscle relaxant I was given. Unfortunately, I didn't mention feeling sick on the ward and spent the next 8 hours vomiting everything I had eaten (one cheese sandwich all day) and drank (including water). By 11pm, an ambulance was called to the house, and once again I was surrounded (semi-naked in bed) by my wife, son and paramedics. Fortunately, this time I started to improve and did not need to back to hospital.

As it was a Friday, I spent the whole weekend worried about the "non stent", gradually becoming more convinced they had "missed" the circumflex until we rang the consultant's secretary on Monday. We were told "no further action required … at this time.". I don't know what that means for the future, but for the moment I only have one stent and still have some blockages (in key arteries). I am waiting for a follow-up with the consultant and hopefully will get some answers then.

Recovery has been a slow process and I have not returned to the supermarket, not because I am physically unable to, but the emotional trauma has really taken its toll on me (and the whole family). On the plus side, while I have been recovering, I finished my dog behaviour book, which is now available on Amazon, and I am currently writing my heart story (which hopefully will be published soon).

I stayed in touch with the chaps from the hospital and have found a wonderful Facebook community for survivors and their families. Emotional support is not always offered as part of rehab, and these types of connections (with people in similar situations) really help with the aftermath of a serious heart event.

The Early Days of the Roller Coaster

When I first heard the words 'we think you're having a heart attack' I just laughed and made some kind of joke about preferring to have a stomach ulcer. I was in denial and shock, not to mention surprise but I wasn't scared.

Later at the first hospital I was still not really taking it in, in fact, it didn't make any sense to me at all. Even when laying in the Cath Lab having emergency clot-busting and 3 stents, I just thought it was a run of the mill kind of medical issue. I was even told to stop talking by my cardiologist as I kept moving and I still had my weird gallows humour. I think it must have the amount of fentanyl I was given that stopped me from processing what was happening.

But then as I was recovering in the High Dependency Unit, I started to hear the words echo around my head. I was still trying to make sense of what had happened and what it meant to my life. Again, in denial I just thought I would get home, have a couple or three days' rest and then be tickety-boo again, notwithstanding having a leg in a plaster cast!

How wrong I was, the enormity hit me when I got home and the meaning of the words that had been used scared the hell out of me (that's me being polite).

How did you feel when you heard these words?
Arrhythmia
Blood pressure
Cardiac arrest
Cardiac rehabilitation
Cardiologist
Defect
Heart attack
Heart bypass
Heart disease
Heart failure
Heart surgery
Stents and balloons
Valve replacement

Yes, they are all frightening words when you consider the implications, aren't they? They don't have to be though. In this book I help you work through all of the "stuff", the "things" and the "feelings" that can often be overlooked and not understood by those around us.

Initially, when I left the hospital, I felt elated and free, looking forward to picking up where I left off and getting on with life. How wrong I was. I wasn't home long before I was to become aware of just how much life had changed, how much my mind had dealt with and how much my body had suffered.

For me, the emotional and mental reaction happened really fast. Perhaps because I was already incapacitated by having a ruptured Achilles tendon, maybe because it was such an emergency who knows. I did learn that not everyone gets hit by this freight train of emotions at the same time.

My dad had a heart attack in August 2020, when he came home, he seemed fine and even quite chipper. He couldn't understand why I was so attentive and concerned about how he felt. But, sure enough, about 4 weeks later it hit him too. He lost his energy, motivation and confidence. He was stressed, he was tired, he was sad and he was angry.

I have since learnt that many people go through this and sometimes it can be as long as 3 months later. I do hope you are one of the lucky few that don't go through this grieving process or if you do it only touches you lightly. The most important words I can say are: **You are not alone!**

Emotional cardiac rehabilitation

Everyone is different everyone is unique so all of our experiences, thoughts, beliefs, feelings and responses are without a doubt going to be different. The one thing we all have in common is that it is a journey and that there is no final destination. That's probably not what you wanted to hear but it is the truth. Another truth is that it is not going to always be in the same direction, there may be twists and turns, you may need to reverse or even turn around sometimes. Recovery from the emotional impact of a cardiac event or heart health diagnosis is a process.

What I want you to hold on to is that you can enjoy the journey and remember that your life has always been about change. Change is one of the constants in life.

Change /chānj/
Definition from Oxford's English Dictionary

Verb

- make (someone or something) different; alter or modify.
- replace (something) with something else, especially something of the same kind that is newer or better; substitute one thing for (another).

Noun

- an act or process through which something becomes different.

The majority of people don't feel comfortable with change (and that may be an understatement). If you have recently had a cardiac event or been given a cardiac health diagnosis the changes have been almost instantaneous, with very little if any warning, are unexpected and are life-threatening. I used changes rather than change as it isn't just the interventions that cause a change in our lives but our thoughts, feelings and beliefs with the additional life changes to reduce our risk factors. The loss of our old life, the old ways of being and the realisation that we are not immortal or invincible.

Grief /grēf/
Definition from Merriam-Webster's Dictionary

Noun

- deep and poignant distress caused by or as if by bereavement
- a cause of such suffering

As I mentioned, when I got home my world became a rollercoaster ride of emotions. Some days I just sat and wept, I couldn't say why I was crying but I felt such grief, such loss, and so alone. It would happen randomly for what seemed like no reason at all. At first, I tried to pull myself together and 'just get over it'. That didn't help as when it didn't work it just made me feel worse as I felt I had no control of myself. I could divert my attention for a little while but the sadness would come back again and it felt like it would never change.

I felt like I was grieving, grieving the loss of my life, my lost future, the loss of trust in my body and the loss of being myself. I swung from feeling irritable on some days, anxious on others. Continually worrying about the slightest change in my body, I had breathlessness, palpitations and felt panic from time to time. I had brain fog, I felt lost, I was super sensitive, lost confidence felt ashamed and embarrassed, I felt guilty and depressed. Would it ever end?

Yes, it did.

It was reading a book completely called "The Luck Factor" that made me start to think differently. I suddenly realised that I was going through a bereavement and it made unexpected multiple changes to my life that I hadn't signed up for.

It triggered a thought to go back and refresh my memory of the change curve and grief model that I used with clients when I was coaching and doing therapy work. I am now going to share this with you as whilst it won't change how you are feeling it will help you understand that it is perfectly normal to feel the way you do, that there are stages that you will go through, maybe not just the once and that there is a future that will feel much better than it does right now.

Grief change curve

The Change Curve model was created by Elisabeth Kubler-Ross. She was a Swiss physician/researcher who identified the process while working with terminally ill patients.

She first introduced it in her 1969 book "On Death and Dying". She describes five stages of emotional and psychological response to grief, tragedy and catastrophic loss.

These stages are not necessarily experienced in a linear progression and not all stages are experienced by all those who grieve.

It was found that her model was valid in the majority of situations relating to change in general. The Kubler-Ross Change Curve is also effectively used by business leaders to help their workforce adapt to change and move towards success.

Experiences of change

Buying your first home, moving house, starting a new job or being made redundant, the breakdown of a relationship or meeting someone new, loss of a loved one, serious health issues, having your first child, going on holiday; It's all change and these are some of the bigger life changers and some of them are positive but still create unease. Something small like changing your supermarket is change but at a different level and can still create feelings of frustration and confusion. The only thing that is constant is change; big or small if you stop and notice you can begin to see the constant shift around us. It is the truth of life; change is a process, it's not something that has a specific beginning and a finite end. It's a journey we move through changing as we progress. We all move at different speeds through this journey.

The rollercoaster of the heart and mind

The model that I show you and describe in the following pages is not the original Kubler-Ross Change Curve but it is very similar. It is my take on how having a cardiac event, heart surgery or diagnosis impacts our thoughts, feelings and behaviours. It is blended with other key needs to help you through change.

By understanding your feelings and emotions it will help you deal with each phase of the curve and be able to celebrate as you move towards it. Going through change will feel quite a lot like stepping outside your comfort zone.

If you look at the diagram of the curve, can you pinpoint where you are at this moment in time?

Remember change is the only constant. It is very important to bear in mind that you can't and won't stay fixed in any one position. Just like a rollercoaster on its track, you may find that you rock back and forth through the curve until you get enough momentum.

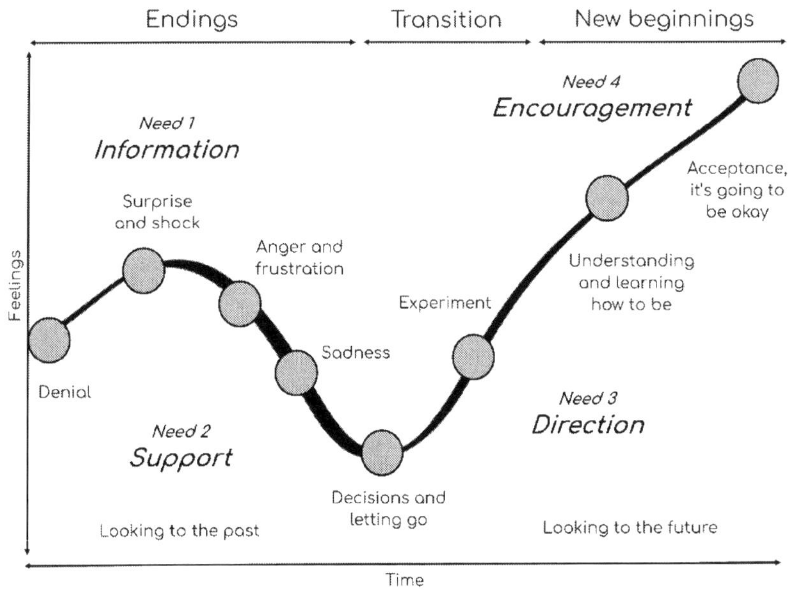

Here are some examples of how you might be thinking and feeling during the early days of your recovery; at the time of the event, surgery or diagnosis.

Initially, you may feel disorientation, and have the thought like "this can't be happening to me". You may experience brain fog, tiredness and muddled sensation. This can affect even the most well organised and prepared person. You may feel confused, a bit lost and insecure.

Being in denial is a protective response, where you might deny the reality of what's happened and the changes you need to make. I couldn't accept that I had heart disease, my heart was healthy, I was fit, I had exercised for the best part of my life and I ate a healthy diet. I believed that the past was perfect and that it was my genetics, not me.

Then it hits you, the shock, the enormity of what has happened to you and your body. It is a catastrophic and sudden loss of the life you had planned and your beliefs about who you are. Who would have thought that you would have a heart condition!

I am not going to go into details here but there is strong evidence that demonstrates that a cardiac event can cause Post Traumatic Stress Disorder (PTSD) in a percentage of cases. If you think you may be experiencing this and you are some months into your recovery then do talk to your medical team, doctor or health practitioner.

Then there are the feelings of anger, ranging anywhere from irritability, some grumblings to full-on rage. It is often misdirected at the people you care about the most or completely undirected and everyone is game. I can remember thinking "why is everyone so blinking (insert your own expletive) slow, I could die before I get where I am going". I rarely if ever have road rage but I did that day.
You might find yourself bargaining; these are unrealistic attempts to get out of the situation. For instance, "if I do this, perhaps the change/s need not happen?" It could be "if you take your cholesterol reducing tablets then you can still eat burgers and take-outs every day". In my case, it was "if I start running then I can go back to martial arts" (Karate is not a good exercise for me as it is too explosive for my heart and my Achilles tendon). No matter what it is and no matter how unrealistic, it will seem reasonable at the time.

It is very common to experience anxiety and/or panic attacks.

These are often based on a realistic fear of the unknown. Other times it will be around the "worst-case scenario' you create in your imagination. You might have a fear of going to sleep in case something happens and you can't do anything. Maybe you fear leaving the house even if it's to go out for a meal. Perhaps you worry about being on your own and not being able to get help. You could be concerned that if you exercise your heart won't be able to cope. You are acutely aware of every twinge in your chest wondering if there is something wrong. These are all normal and have been thought about by many others who have been through a similar experience as you.

I have already spoken about my sadness; this was crying tears and this is again a common reaction and it is healthy and healing. It is not weakness; it is just part of the process; it is healing and healthy. On the other hand, sadness can be expressed as silence and melancholy.

I am not talking about clinical depression but of what I call circumstantial depressed feelings. It is caused by something that has happened and it is felt for short periods of time but may repeat from time to time. You may find yourself feeling down, having no energy, being unengaged and thinking "why bother". If you notice you feel this way remind yourself that it is okay, that all feelings pass, choose to be kind to yourself and acknowledge that you have been through a lot and after a cardiac intervention your body is expending a lot of energy healing itself. You may find yourself sleeping a lot too.

IMPORTANT: *If you have suicidal thoughts or think about harming yourself then get help immediately. Call your emergency services, speak to your doctor or contact a mental health charity.*

Influence on our ability to move to letting go

How you react to change and the effects it has can vary

enormously. What may seem obvious and exciting to you can be scary and pointless to others and vice versa. By taking time to accept the change, understanding what happens to you and the processes you could possibly go through, you'll feel a little more in control and normal.

You will feel more able to deal with the changes needed in your life and the feelings along the way and will be happier, more motivated and more confident. You will feel mentally and emotionally more resilient.

There are often four main areas of needs and feelings that require fulfilling so that you can let go and move on up the curve. They contribute to how you react to the change in your life and they can be summed up as the following:

1. A feeling of insecurity or fear of what the future holds. The feeling of anxiety and stress as in the absence of information and understanding, you will make up your own story and fear the worst. The future chapters in this book were created to give you information and help you understand the changes you need to make and how to actually make them.

2. A sense of unfairness. This is a childlike (not childish) response which you can experience. When something happens that we are not expecting that makes a huge difference the psychological contract we enter into with either our bodies, our minds or other people is sometimes bent or broken. Why did this happen to you? To you, this is not fair.

3. A feeling of powerlessness. It can feel like you have little or no control over events, appointments or the changes you need to make. This can trigger your fight or flight response. In some cases, becoming passive and in others, you may try to take some control back in challenging ways. "You don't think I matter. Well, I'm going to show you that I do!"

4. A lack of reason why. I found myself searching for reasons why I had had my heart attack, I wanted answers but alas there was nothing specific that I could hang it on. It was my lifestyle and some genetics. For me, this is part of being able to start letting go. If you don't understand why or if you feel you need to know a reason, you are not able to motivate yourself to move forwards to the bright new future and you will dig your heels in and stay where you are.

Moving through as quickly and easily as appropriate for you

I am sure that you, just like I, don't want to be in the painful first part of the curve for very long. But it is important to remember that this journey serves a good purpose as it is your mind trying to keep you safe (protect you from danger) while your heart has time to heal and your life adjusts to the necessary changes.

Don't forget that we are all unique and we will all move through at our own pace that is right for us. Try not to get into comparing yourself with others, they are not you and their heart condition is not the same as yours. There are some ways to help you move through the first part of the change curve quicker. So here are my thoughts and suggestions.

You will need factual information, if it is not freely given then take action to find out more. Ask questions, research, ask friends and family, doctors, solicitors, employers. Try to keep your imagination under control, that is unless it is a super amazing future that you see.

Understanding and clarity help you to move through the curve and be able to recognise what is happening. If you don't understand, ask more questions.

Find out how and where to get help from; it may not be where you think it will come from. Be open and aware, there are face to face support groups; they may not be your cup of tea, but try it, you never know and just once might be all you need. There is online support too, Facebook has many groups and there is one, in particular, that was a lifesaver (literally) for me. The British Hearties: Worldwide Hearties Survivors Support Group and not forgetting my own, The My Heart & Mind Community. Then there is telephone support too, many heart health charities have their own helplines.

Make sure you communicate your needs as others can't help you if they don't understand what you need or want. Be as clear and concise as you can and make sure you don't overwhelm people; it is a learning curve for everyone that is involved.

How does it feel to move up the curve?

You may experience confusion and doubt and this is a good sign as you are beginning to move on. Signs of acceptance will begin to shine through, as you may start to ask questions about the future. It is now time for you to take an active role to reframe your experience, find the benefits of the changes and be able to live your life happy. If you experience a setback, it's okay. Allow yourself to accept and realise it is part of the process.

Gently you will notice acceptance and understanding. You'll begin to stop focusing on what you have lost, learn to let go and accept the change. You will then begin to experiment, start exploring what it all means and find ways to adapt to the new reality. It's time to begin to notice what's good and not so good about your heart health and life. Maybe you'll start considering new ideas, new ways of doing things and solutions. Again, any time you find you're slipping back towards doubt remind yourself that this is quite normal and give yourself space to come back to acceptance again.

As you shift and begin to take ownership of the change you will begin to find more solutions for any problems in the new situation. Not only will you be adapting and accepting the change to your life, body and mind but you may surprise yourself and find that you start to embrace it. This is where you will start to see the benefits and rewards of the change as new ideas and pathways in your life begin to flourish.

Without even realising it you will then have found the beginnings of your 'new you' or the early stages of routine and status quo.

"Knowing is not enough! You must take action."

Tony Robbins

Our Nearest & Dearest, Friends & Family

Heart disease is a family affair. When you have a cardiac event or heart disease diagnosis it can really hit those that we love too. Yet they rarely get any support or understanding and sometimes they get the brunt of our sadness, anxiety, depression or anger.

The one thing that you have that they don't is some semblance of control. This is because it is happening to you. You are involved in the treatment and whilst it is scary and full of unknowns you are aware of your own feelings and how your body feels.

In some cases, especially during the COVID-19 pandemic, they haven't been able to attend the hospital with you. They have no idea of what is going on, they want to know what is happening.? How is this going to affect you? What is the treatment? Foremost in their minds are you dead or alive?

They are most likely scared and feel out of control. Their bodies are coursing with cortisol, which is the fight or flight hormone. It's released when danger is perceived, it makes you want to do something to reduce the risk but they can't, all they can do is wait. When I had my heart attack in 2016 but still my father had to wait for hours until I came out of the Cath Lab. He had followed the ambulance to the hospital all blue lights flashing and hadn't seen me since, he just had to wait and wait and wait, he was alone.

Maybe they feel guilt perhaps if they had encouraged you to quit smoking, change your diet or take more exercise, then this wouldn't have happened. I know my friend, Martin, felt very guilty as he had asked me if I wanted to go to A&E three times between Friday and Monday. Each time I said, nope I am okay maybe tomorrow if the indigestion doesn't go away, I don't want to waste their time. He said to me 'if only I had made you go' then you wouldn't have a damaged heart muscle. Despite the knowledge that no way in the world could he have made me, he still felt guilt and that perhaps he could have done more.

They may feel sadness as they know that you now have a serious health issue and it is going to change your life. It will also change theirs in ways that they can't comprehend at first but soon becomes evident as time goes on. Like you, their future has changed, is changing and they need a little time to adjust and create a new vision.

It is quite possible that they may feel some anger too. I know my 14-year-old daughter was very angry at me when I came home. It was borne out of her own fear and panic. I looked so unwell. How would I be able to look after her as I was so ill? What if I was to die, what if I had another heart attack? She wouldn't know what to do. She had lost her idea of our future. It is quite possible that your loved one feels anger at you for not taking care of yourself, maybe not getting medical attention when you needed it or maybe just at the world in general.

It might mean that your roles in the home will change. Perhaps you were the primary breadwinner and cannot go back to your old job. Your partner may need to take on the role of a full-time wage-earner. If they are already working then they may feel greater pressure to keep up the household income.

Maybe like me you are a single parent, my daughter's role changed dramatically, for a long time she became my caregiver as well doing her GCSEs and carrying the worry of losing me. Young children who were used to rough play with you will need to realise that such play is over for now and they may feel like it's their fault.

Surprisingly, some of the friends that I thought would be there for me after my heart attack just disappeared. Some only sent me a text message wishing me well but didn't get in touch again. This was heart breaking for me, very upsetting and made me feel even more alone and helpless. In hindsight now I realise that maybe the reality was that they just didn't know what to say. It could be that my heart attack brought home their own mortality, that they felt scared and didn't want to say the wrong thing.
The flip side of this was that 'my people' were there, they sent flowers, called over, they sent messages and cards. The best thing though was that 'my people' were not only my besties but also people that were acquaintances that have become really close to me. And some were total strangers at the time they just happened across my path and we have become firm friends.

To talk or not to talk, that is the question. Do you have an avoidant way of coping, would you really rather not think about your heart health diagnosis? Does it feel better to shut it out of your mind and just carry on with what you were doing before? This can be very difficult for your family; they may find this distressing because they think you need to talk about it.

They also want to know what's going on for you physically and emotionally, they want to help and they want to have some control to ease their fear.

You may find that everyone does everything for you regardless of if you want it or can do it. It's part of their care and love for you but sometimes it can make you feel useless and unempowered. Try to hold in mind that they just want to help and they quite literally want to look after you.

Communication is the key to keeping families and relationships emotionally healthy. They need you to help them to help you. Everyone needs to talk honestly about what they're feeling, this includes children as they can blame themselves when their parents fall ill.

By talking things out initially it helps resolve stress and promotes intimacy and emotional support. I suggest that you have a conversation and discuss how your heart health has impacted you, them and your life together.

Explain to them what you need from them and acknowledge what they might need from you.

This next chapter is written for your caregivers and family. Please do share it with them as I hope it helps prompt some conversations and for you to live your life happy.

"The love of family and friends is the glue that holds your heart together."

Jennifer Betts

You Can Help Me!

After a cardiac event, having stents, pacemakers and other bits fitted isn't the fix that most people think. It's only the beginning of a long road back to recovery. Both the survivors and their loved ones need support and understanding. The event can and indeed does change not only survivor's lives, but the lives of those around and close to them.

With the best will in the world, you try to help someone you love and care about. You want to support your cardiac warrior. But it doesn't always go the way you planned. Sometimes you may think that your words and actions will make your loved one feel better, when in fact they get more upset, frustrated or angry. Your intention is always good and yet it leaves you feeling like nothing you can say or do will help.

In 2016 I ruptured my Achilles tendon, had a heart attack and was diagnosed with breast cancer. I had my moments where no one could do right for doing wrong. Here are some ideas to help you, help us as we are in this together.

"How are you feeling?

You want to know how we are; you genuinely care and are interested but sometimes we just don't want to talk. So, you will get an "I'm OK" response. We appreciate your care and know that you are there when and if we want to talk, but sometimes it's hard if you ask the question frequently and push us to know more.

How you can help … It's a delicate balance I'm afraid. You need to just be there for us, we will share with you when we are ready and we appreciate your support. Try to treat us as you did before our diagnosis and let it go if we say "I'm fine". As a partner one needs to be very careful as on the other hand, you don't want to act as if nothing has happened.

"You look really well!"

At a guess, I would say that you want us to feel great and that things are improving. You are complimenting us and want to raise our spirits.

However, just because we 'look good doesn't mean we feel good'. Like many of the invisible diseases what we look like on the outside doesn't match with how we are feeling inside physically and emotionally.

How you can help … when you say things like 'You're looking great" you have a positive intention to make the person feel good. Do make sure that you also acknowledge that they may not feel 100%.

"You should get out walking or go to the gym"

Again, your intention is a good one, you are hoping to motivate us to get out there and strengthen our bodies. Dr Shad Helmstetter explains that when we tell ourselves or others that they "should" be doing something, we're implicitly reinforcing the idea that they're not doing it. This then makes us demotivated and feel like a failure.

How you can help … suggest doing something with us, going for a walk or joining an exercise class, you can encourage us to do with you.

"You mustn't eat that!"
We do know you are trying to protect us from making the wrong food choices. You want us to be fit and healthy. To us, we feel like we have no choice, it's a bridge too far and it feels like nagging.

How you can help ... understand that everything in moderation is fine. Help us find alternatives that still give us satisfaction. Change your choices with us; if it's not in the house then we can't eat it.

"What's wrong?"
You want to help us and you don't know why we are feeling and acting the way we do. We will have good and bad days and sometimes we haven't a clue why or what's wrong. It's just how we are.

How you can help .... Accept and expect that it will happen and might be for quite a while. Acknowledge that we aren't feeling chipper and remind us to be kind to ourselves and that it will pass in time.

"Don't be silly; what are you worrying about?"
For you, it does seem silly, especially if it is something we used to do without batting an eyelid. You really want us to see that it's nothing to worry about, but to us, even the little things seem impossible and our confidence is at an all-time low. Our bodies have let us down, we have let our bodies down and everything is different now.

In the first few months after my heart attack, I wouldn't leave the house. Eventually, my best friend, Dot, persuaded me to go out for lunch. Even then I would only eat in a restaurant directly opposite my doctor's surgery.

How you can help .... be aware that what is 'simples' for you may not be to us as we are recovering. There is no time limit when everything goes back to normal. We are trying to work out our new normal! Help us take it one step at a time, my dad always says 'inch by inch is a synch, yard by yard is hard'. Baby steps and we will get there with your support and encouragement.

"Why are you always tired?"

This is something that I really didn't understand before I had a heart attack and cancer. You probably don't either; you can see we sleep a lot and expect us to have energy but we don't.

It's something that I just can't explain but it is fatigue, tiredness and lethargy like I have never known before. No matter how many hours of sleep I get I still feel tired. It could be due to the damage to my heart, it could be emotional exhaustion, and it might be my body and mind still healing. We also take medication that slows our heart rate and lowers our blood pressure. We also experience difficulty sleeping and staying asleep.

How you can help ... There isn't a lot that can make a difference but asking us why or telling us to go to bed early doesn't help. It may be fatigue and it's not a sleep deficit that causes that but how much energy the body is using healing itself. It does a lot of healing while we are asleep which is why we do sleep quite a lot. Make sure we tell our doctor and that we get blood tests to check our vitamin D and iron levels. Understanding can make a real difference as we are often just as irritated ourselves.

"Come on eat something!"

Initially, for a few months, my appetite completely disappeared. My friends and family kept on trying to feed me up as a sign of love. It just frustrated me and made me feel bad to waste food.

How you can help ... be patient with us. Give us only small quantities of food. This can help as it means we are not overwhelmed by the amount of food on the plate. If we do finish it, it feels like a complete meal – what we see, an empty plate makes us feel good.

"Stop being so picky or a perfectionist!"
Sometimes when we have a good day, we can do many things and feel that we do them well, but when we are having a not so good day, these things can be impossible. We feel frustrated when we know we used to be able to do something and now we can't. It is difficult and we aren't happy if it is not the way we wanted it. Our inability to do things that we used to do affects our well-being. We need to have purpose and value in our lives and to feel achievement.

How you can help … just understand, don't try and make it better as nothing can make it better other than time or acceptance for us. The physical and emotional changes caused by a heart attack or other cardiac event can have a huge impact. Let us know you are there for us and will happily help if needed and asked.

"I just don't understand you!"
Post heart attack I realised that unless you go through it the impact of a heart attack is unimaginable, as are many other life-changing events. I was supported by wonderful friends and family; I know it wasn't easy for them. Many years ago, one of my closest friends, Ian, had a heart attack. When I visited him in hospital, I appreciated that he was really ill but thought that once he was home, he was OK. Since my own heart attack and recovery, I now understand this is so not the case. I watched my friends and family try to understand as I became anxious, scared and lost confidence.

How you can help … Listen, actively listen, sometimes we just need to be heard. You don't have to give us the answers as sometimes there aren't any, we really want to know we are not alone.

Support for you as a loved one
It could help to join one or all of these Facebook groups. I have included the group description for you. These do change so make sure you visit the group about me tab.

There are many more active groups on Facebook, add heart or cardiac to the search function and you'll find them. Here is the about information at the time of writing this book.

My Heart & Mind Community
www.facebook.com/groups/mindheartandmindcommunity

You are welcome if you have had a heart attack, cardiac event or life with a heart disease diagnosis, this group is for you. This community is for people who have experience of a cardiac event and are having difficulty managing the emotional side of rehabilitation. Primarily this group is a safe and nurturing place for you (and your partner) if you have had heart-related problems such as a heart attack, transplant, cardiac arrest or have been diagnosed with heart disease etc.

The purpose is to support each other to adjust to our lives during a time of shock, panic, anxiety, sleeplessness, anger, fatigue, lack of energy, sadness and confusion. There are many changes that are needed to be made to your life. I help you create the mindset that enables you to make the necessary lifestyle changes that reduce your risk and most importantly manage your thoughts and feelings. This group is for people who want to learn the art of feeling happy despite heart disease.

British Hearties: Worldwide Hearties Survivors Support Group
www.facebook.com/groups/1698204250451010

Welcome to British Hearties: Worldwide hearties survivors support group. This group is for anyone who has had a Heart Attack, Heart Transplant, Sudden Cardiac Arrest or been diagnosed with heart disease, Cardiomyopathy or any other Heart related problems. Family members are welcome. The purpose of the group is to support each other, share heart-healthy tips, share news and information about heart disease and discuss health.

Heart Attack Families and Friends Group
www.facebook.com/groups/Heartattackfamiliesandfriends

We are a little group of people who have suffered from heart attacks or any heart problems. We are also a group of people who are the partners and guardians and friends of people who have suffered from some form of heart disease. The group is designed to help one another through the good and bad times. To make new friends who may have the same problems. Also, to discuss issues that we may all have and sometimes to have a bloody good laugh and sometimes a damn good moan.

All in all, there is no right or wrong thing to say or do. I've made a few suggestions that I wish I had been able to share when I was feeling fragile and unwell.

If you're still reading this, I hope this helps you. At the least, it will have given you a reminder that everything that people say and do comes from a good place and is because they care.

If you are a confused friend or member of the family, I hope that this gives you an idea of what is going on for us; how we may be feeling and thinking. Ultimately, I hope it helps to communicate all our needs and save those awkward moments.

Appointment Preparation

After a heart disease diagnosis, there are many appointments at both hospitals and medical centres. There are also specialist appointments such as your diabetes nurse, INR (international normalized ratio) tests, dietician and your rehab team. They can all seem rather daunting and worrying at times. We can experience a loss of control at this point. You can also have a case of white coat syndrome and we feel we can't ask questions or challenge information given to us by those that are in charge.

Your recovery and wellbeing both pragmatically and emotionally are about you having confidence in yourself and the people caring for you medically. I would recommend always using a charm offensive. The following definitely set me up for success along the way and the key was about building relationships.

Build a great relationship with your cardiologist, their secretary and your GP. Make friends with your other specialists, your cardiac rehab team, PT instructor, diabetes nurse and pharmacist.

Always prepare in advance for appointments and make sure that you ask questions to ensure your understanding. You are the most important person in your recovery. Attend all of your appointments where possible and always let them know in advance if you can't make one. Never cancel an appointment without remaking a future one, it's amazing how quickly you can forget to do it later.

Ask for help if needed. Ask questions, even the ones that you think are daft, I can pretty much guarantee you aren't the only person wondering the same thing. Remember these people are on your side, they are trying to keep you alive not make your life a misery.

A basic plan can help you make the most of your appointment whether you are meeting with your doctor, your cardiologist or your cardiac rehabilitation team. The following ideas will make it easier for you and your medical team to cover everything you need to talk about. It is worth keeping a note of them day by day. If something occurs to you, capture your thoughts and write them down so you remember to include them in your discussions.

Keep an appointment journal

Use the journal pages at the end of this chapter. Capture your thoughts, feelings and medical questions or physical experiences. Just jot them down when you think or notice something. For example, do you have a new symptom you want to ask the doctor about? Are you concerned about how a treatment is affecting your daily life?

It can be hard to remember things when you are sitting in front of your doctor so keeping a record in between appointments, make sure you get all the answers you want. Sometimes you may find that as you are reviewing them you no longer need to mention it.

Make notes or create a list and prioritise your concerns

From your journal notes, you can make an appointment notes list of what you want to discuss. You can find a form for this at the end of this chapter too.

If you have more than a few items to discuss, put them in order and ask about the most important ones first. Don't put off the things that are really on your mind until the end of your appointment as you may run out of time. Make sure you bring them up right away!

Information to take with you

I would always recommend that you make a list of all your medications. That means everything you take and the dose. This includes all your prescription drugs, over-the-counter medicines, vitamins and herbal remedies or supplements.

If appropriate, depending on what country you are in, you should take your most current insurance cards, with each one's contact information included to ensure payment for the doctor's services, ordered treatments and prescriptions will be paid efficiently. You may need to take with you the names and telephone numbers of other doctors you see and your medical records if the doctor doesn't already have them.

Consider having family or a friend with you

Sometimes it is helpful to bring a family member or close friend with you. Let them know in advance what you want from your visit. Your companion can remind you of what you wanted to discuss in case you forget. They can also take notes for you, to help you remember what the practitioner said. Don't let your companion take too strong a role. For the best results, let your companion know in advance how they can help the most.

Bring them up to date

Let your doctor know what has happened in your life since your last visit. If you have been treated in the emergency room or by a specialist, tell the doctor right away. Mention any changes you have noticed in your appetite, weight, sleep, or energy level. Also, tell them about any recent changes in any medications you take or the effects they have had on you.

Be sure you can see and hear

Remember to take your glasses with you. If you have a hearing aid, make sure that it is working well and wear it.

Always let the doctor know if you have a hard time seeing or hearing.

At the beginning of the appointment, it might be helpful to say something like the following:

'My hearing makes it hard to understand everything you're saying. It helps a lot when you speak slowly and face me when you're talking.'

Don't get fed up waiting

Sometimes appointments get delayed and it can be frustrating even though you know it is likely there is good reason for it. Having something pleasant to keep your mind occupied in busy waiting rooms can make the wait better. Bring along a book, magazines or a crossword book.

Make sure you have a fully-charged mobile phone and take along headphones to listen to favourite music, podcast, audio book or to stream movies.

Keep hydrated and don't get hangry

As I mentioned it is not uncommon to have a delay even with a scheduled appointment. There can be health emergency situations, your medical practitioner might get behind and you may be required to wait for lab or test results, this can extend an appointment.

Providing you aren't asked to fast before or during your appointment, consider bringing some sustenance. Include some bottled water and easy-to-eat healthy snacks for fast energy boosts.

If not allowed to have food in the centre or while you are being assessed, have it ready in your car for when you're finished.

The full picture

If you have had serious wounds from surgery, health conditions or other reasons, it can be a good idea to take pictures on your mobile phone during the healing stages while at home. This can help give a more accurate view of how you have been doing. It's also a good idea to keep a list of any possible signs of infection and any adverse symptoms that are not always present during appointments.

Make it easy on yourself

There are some other practical and simple ways to better prepare for an upcoming medical appointment. Dress comfortably in looser clothing, comfy shoes and remove most jewellery before leaving home to avoid losing them.

Ask questions

Don't hesitate to ask questions and voice concerns as they occur to you during the appointment. There really are no stupid questions, it's your body and you who needs to understand the plan, what's happening and any other details.

It's okay to ask for clarity if you don't understand something. Make sure you write down the answers.

It's a good idea to capture any questions that come up in between your appointments. These will be personal to you and your situation, but here are a few that you might want to ask at an initial appointment with your cardiologist or cardiac rehab team.

- How does my family history affect my heart health?
- Is my blood pressure reading normal?
- What is my cholesterol level, how does this affect my heart?

- Am I experiencing a heart symptom due to my age, gender, or weight?
- Are my symptoms indicating heart disease?
- Are my eating habits causing my heart symptoms?
- Are my exercise habits causing my heart symptoms?
- Is my level of stress/anxiety increasing my risk of heart complications?
- What are my treatment options for the heart symptoms I am having?
- What should I do if my symptoms persist?

Get a recap

Before leaving your appointment, ask for a recap. Ask the doctor to repeat the instructions you're supposed to follow and make sure you're both on the same page. Again, make sure you write things down, so you can remember what you talked about later.

Be sure you know how to contact them if you have further questions and if you are supposed to let them have any feedback about how the treatment is going.

"Confidence is preparation. Everything else is beyond your control."

Richard Kline

Appointment Journal (part 1)

Your general health topics for discussion, remember to include a date when adding to your comments. *Some suggestions angina symptoms, bowel problems, chest pain, feeling dizzy, feeling lightheaded, headaches, medications, muscular pain or stiffness, pain or discomfort or shortness of breath.*

Your lifestyle and risk factors topics for discussion, remember to include a date when adding to your comments. *Some suggestions might be alcohol, appetite changes, blood pressure, cholesterol, diabetes, exercise, medicines, nutrition & diet, smoking and weight changes*

DOWNLOAD: www.myheartandmind.co.uk/bookTBGO

Appointment Journal (part 2)

Your thoughts and feelings topics for discussion, remember to include a date when adding to your comments. *Some suggestions, feeling anxious, agitation or angry, feeling lonely or isolated, feeling sad, down, or blue, intimacy or sexual activity, memory or thinking problems, seep problems or changes in sleep patterns.*

Anything else that comes to mind that you don't want to forget.

DOWNLOAD: www.myheartandmind.co.uk/bookTBGO

Appointment Notes

Doctor	Specialty	Date and Time

Appointment notes and questions to discuss. Take these from your appointment journal notes. List them in your order of priority from most important to least important.
1
2
3
4
5
6
7
8
9
10

DOWNLOAD: www.myheartandmind.co.uk/bookTBGO

Managing Medications

Following a cardiac event or heart disease diagnosis, you may be prescribed some or all of the following medication to reduce your risk of having another cardiac event. This is called secondary prevention medication.

Even when you feel better you will still benefit from taking most of these medications. You will get the benefits for as long as you take them so you may be on these medicines for life.

How medication helps

No one, I know, likes taking medicines but they are a critical part of staying well when living with heart disease.

They help to reduce your risk of a future heart attack, arrest, angina, heart failure and stroke. They help to manage your symptoms and improve your quality of life by keeping you out of the hospital. They help you to live longer. It's important to remember that you may be given different medicines to do different things. You will need to take most of your medicines long term.

Before discharge, you will receive specific information about your medications from the ward nurse. Your cardiologist, along with your doctor, will decide the best medicines for you to take at home to help you manage your heart condition.

Your medications will also be discussed during the cardiac rehabilitation programme.

When you leave the hospital, you will only have enough medicine for a short time. It is important that you keep taking these medicines. Make sure you see your doctor for more prescriptions before you run out.

Some dos about taking your medicines

- ✓ Do carry a list of your medicines, doses and instructions for taking them. I have this in my emergency contact details on my mobile phone.
- ✓ Do check with your doctor or pharmacist before taking over-the-counter or complementary medicines (e.g., cold and flu medicine, vitamins or herbs).
- ✓ Do make sure you see your doctor regularly to check that your medicines are working properly.
- ✓ Do take your medicines exactly as your doctor advises. Get into a routine, this will help you create a new habit.
- ✓ Do talk with your doctor or pharmacist about possible side effects. An unexpected reaction to the medication, such as a fever, a rash or diarrhoea.
- ✓ Do try to learn the names of your tablets and understand why you are taking them.
- ✓ Do keep your medication in its own labelled container. Unless you are using weekly pill containers.
- ✓ Do keep medicine out of the reach and sight of children.

Some don'ts about taking your medicines

- × Don't change the doses unless your doctor tells you to.

- ✗ Don't crush or break tablets to make it easier to take them unless the doctor or pharmacist tells you to do this.
- ✗ Don't open capsules to mix the content with a liquid to make it easier to take.
- ✗ Don't run out of your medicines – keep enough of a supply at home.
- ✗ Don't stop taking your medicine, even if you feel well, without first consulting your doctor first.
- ✗ Don't take medicine that's past its 'use by' or 'best before' date.
- ✗ Don't take someone else's medication, even if it has the same name as yours.

Having trouble taking medicines?
If you have trouble taking your medicine (eg. you can't swallow the tablets or opening the medicine bottle is difficult), speak to your doctor or pharmacist immediately. They will help find a solution – medicines can be changed or repackaged.

A quick tip is to take medicines of the same shape and size together and take them with plenty of liquid.

Organising your medicines
It is quite common for people to forget when to take their medicine or have difficulty taking their medicine. Especially in the early days when it is all new and confusing. It is important to ask your doctor or pharmacist what to do if you do forget to take your medicine as advised or if you accidentally took it twice.

Make sure you order your pills in enough time. Always double check if you are unsure. Remember it takes time for the prescription to be signed off and then some medications may need ordering and then the prescription gets made up. Make friends with your pharmacist they are important in managing your health.

If you find it difficult to remember when to take your medicine, speak to your pharmacist about packaging it into an easy-to-follow medicine organiser blister pack. Sometimes these are called dosset boxes. These are made up in weeks and usually dispensed four weeks at a time. Sometimes these are free of charge, while some pharmacies have a fee for making them up for you.

If they won't make them up for you and you can't afford the charge, then do it yourself. You can buy pill dispenser boxes from most chemists and pharmacies and online too. Refill your Pill containers just once a month: Invest in a months' worth of weekly pill containers. Then do it yourself monthly. By batching and doing it in bulk it will save you time and will reduce the risk of making daily mistakes.

How to remember to take your medicines

An easy way to build in a new habit is to add it to existing habits, it's called habit stacking. I am really lucky as I only need to take my medications three times a day. Once when I first open my eyes, I have added this to when I get up have a wee and clean my teeth. Then about an hour later, after I have had a shower and make my first cup of coffee. Lastly, before I go to bed at night. I always have a glass of sparkling water, so I take them when I pour my glass, then top it up again. Yay, it increases my water intake as well. That always needs work, so it's a bit of a win/win for me.

There are quite a few online tools to help you keep an up-to-date list of your medicines and remind you when to take them. I haven't tried this myself but I have seen a few people recommend the Medisafe App. It's a free app with an option to upgrade to a paid-for version. They say 'Keeping track of medications is difficult. We can help. Take the stress out of taking your medications. Spend less time thinking about medications and more time living your life'.

If you can't make a connection to a current habit, then create a new one. Think of all the possible ways you can remind yourself when you need to take your medication. Use post-it notes and stick them around your home/office. Use your phone and set an alarm to remind you. With some smartphones and Alexa, you can always say what the reminder is for. It takes 42 days of consecutive behaviour to create a new habit. In the early days, I'd recommend putting an alarm on your phone. You can then relax a little and know (do double check all is set correctly) your phone will call you when it's time to take your meds.

Ask your partner or friend to help you remember. Asking for help from your friends or family for helping with organising your pills or remembering to take them. This is NOT a sign of weakness; this is a sign of courage and commitment to living your life and sharing their future. Being vulnerable is beautiful, it allows others the pleasure of being able to be of service to someone they care about.

A really simple and easy tip is to leave your medication visible (if it is safe to do so). Leave it in view where you usually make yourself a drink.

Alternatively, you can label up some small stacking pots. I used small plastic shot glasses for my mum who was taking her meds seven times a day, all with the times written on the outside with a sticky label.

If they have been provided in blister packs, keep them open so you can see where you are in the day. The same applies to the colourful dispenser packs you can buy via Amazon or pick up in your pharmacy.

If you need accountability why not join and ask for support in a heart-related Facebook group. Everyone within the group will have had a similar experience as you. They will encourage you, remind you and celebrate your announced successes. All this goes toward reinforcing a new habit and as a side effect, you will make new friends. Trust me you'll get feedback that will make you feel really good.

An important part of creating the new neural pathways that are your new habits is to reward yourself. This really embeds the feeling of completion. When you complete a task or activity, your body naturally releases the hormones dopamine (as you strive to achieve) and serotonin (when you get there, you've achieved it). These feel-good chemicals are released to help us do more of what keeps us safe. Let's give them a helping hand by making sure you have something to celebrate your success even after completing it for one day.

Then be ready to rejoice after day 7. Perhaps a different reward, again something simple that makes you smile. It helps to keep a calendar too, you can tick off your days of success, this gives you a streak that you just don't want to break. Keep at it but be prepared for a reward again on day 21, it doesn't have to be something big, maybe just pat yourself on the back, quite literally pat yourself on the back and give yourself a hug of success. Remember that it can take around 42 days of consecutive behaviour to create a new habit, so get prepared for a celebration on that day.

Get to know your medicines

It's important to know what medicine you're taking, what it does and how it might affect you. Your doctor or pharmacist can give you this information, it is also available enclosed with your medications. Always read the labels, leaflets and instructions.

It can sometimes be confusing as often the drug name and brand name are different and some medicines have more than one brand name.

Make sure you follow your doctor and pharmacist's advice about when and how to take your medicines (eg. at a particular time of the day, or with food). It is important to know this as it is crucial to how the medicine works and some may also interact with each other.

There's a useful medication chart at the end of the next chapter that will help you keep a record of what you take when to take it and what it is for.

Possible side effects

It is worth remembering that not everyone will experience these, in the main most medication is well tolerated today. You can find information about this in medication packaging.

If you are concerned then do talk with your doctor as ask what to do if you have side effects. Check if any of your medicines might affect you before driving, operating machinery or doing jobs where you need to be alert.

If you think you feel a medicine side effect, speak with your doctor or pharmacist as soon as you can. Don't stop taking your medicine until you do. Often symptoms are coincidental and due to another cause.

If you do think you are experiencing any side effects it helps to keep a record of it as it is useful when having conversations with your doctors. Keeping a note is great as evidence if you want to build a case to try an alternative medication. It helps you to keep a check on how you're feeling so you can become more aware of the effects.

Common Medicines

The medicines you take depend on your heart condition and symptoms. It is often quite normal to take a number of different kinds of medicines. Medication is important to your recovery as it reduces your risk of future heart events and complications. The medication you are prescribed depends on the cause of your cardiac diagnosis. They have many names and will differ from country to country. You must always take prescribed heart medication and speak with your doctor or pharmacist before making any changes. Here are some of the more common ones:

Anti-clotting (anti-platelet) medicines
These medications help to stop blood clots from forming in your blood vessels. They keep blood clots from forming by preventing blood platelets from sticking together.

You usually need antiplatelet medicines if you've had coronary angioplasty and stent implantation.

Antiplatelet meds help prevent clotting in patients who have had a heart attack, unstable angina, ischemic strokes, TIA (transient ischemic attacks) and other forms of cardiovascular disease. They can also be prescribed preventively when plaque build-up is evident but there is not yet a major blockage in the artery.

If you take an antiplatelet medicine, unless you are suffering severe bleeding you must not stop taking it unless your cardiologist or doctor tells you to. This is even more important if you have had a stent implanted.

Aspirin

It helps to prevent platelets in your blood from sticking together and forming small clots. It is very important to prevent clots from forming in your blood vessels. Aspirin is taken once daily after some food. It should be taken after food to help protect your stomach. Tell your doctor if you experience indigestion after taking aspirin. Another medicine may be prescribed to counteract this. You will need to take aspirin lifelong.

Clopidogrel/Ticagrelor

This is another anti-platelet drug and works together with aspirin to give the best possible cover. This may be prescribed for either 12 months or longer. It is very important that you continue taking this drug as prescribed to prevent small clots from forming in your blood vessels.

Antiplatelet agents that are commonly prescribed include:

- Aspirin
- Clopidogrel (Plavix)
- Dipyridamole (Persantine)
- Prasugrel (Effient)
- Ticagrelor (Brilinta)

Anticoagulant (blood thinner) medicines

Anticoagulant medicines help to prevent blood clots from forming and treat existing clots. They decrease the clotting (coagulating) ability of the blood. Sometimes called blood thinners, although they do not actually thin the blood. They are used to treat certain blood vessel, heart and lung conditions.

Anticoagulants help to prevent harmful clots from forming in the blood vessels. They may prevent the clots from becoming larger and causing more serious problems. They are often prescribed to prevent first or recurrent stroke.

If you are taking this type of medication you need to have regular blood tests to check you're taking the right dose and that it's working properly.

In addition to other medicines, some foods and beverages, alcohol, herbs and vitamins can change how anticoagulant medicines work. Speak to your doctor, nurse or pharmacist about what foods, drinks and supplements can interact with your medication.

Anticoagulant medications commonly prescribed include:

- Apixaban (Eliquis)
- Dabigatran (Pradaxa)
- Edoxaban (Savaysa)
- Heparin (various)
- Rivaroxaban (Xarelto)
- Warfarin (Coumadin)

Blood pressure medicines

Angiotensin-converting enzyme (ACE) inhibitors

ACE inhibitors widen ('dilate') your blood vessels and reduce strain on your heart. They are used to lower blood pressure, make your heart work better and improve your chance of surviving after a heart attack.

They expand blood vessels and decrease resistance by lowering levels of angiotensin II, an enzyme that can cause your blood vessels to constrict. This allows your blood to flow more easily and makes the heart's work easier or more efficient. They are prescribed to treat or improve symptoms of cardiovascular conditions including high blood pressure and heart failure. ACE Inhibitors have been shown to reduce your risk of a further cardiac event.

Angiotensin-Converting Enzyme Inhibitors commonly prescribed include:

- Benazepril (Lotensin)
- Captopril (Capoten)
- Enalapril (Vasotec)
- Fosinopril (Monopril)
- Lisinopril (Prinivil, Zestril)
- Moexipril (Univasc)
- Perindopril (Aceon)
- Quinapril (Accupril)
- Ramipril (Altace)
- Trandolapril (Mavik)

Angiotensin II Receptor Blockers or Inhibitors (also known as ARBs)

ARBs are sometimes used instead of ACE inhibitors if you get side effects, such as a persistent cough, from taking ACE inhibitors. ARBs work like ACE inhibitors - they widen your blood vessels and reduce strain on your heart.

Rather than lowering levels of angiotensin II (as ACE inhibitors do) angiotensin II receptor blockers prevent this chemical from having any effect on the heart and blood vessels. This keeps blood pressure from rising.

These drugs are used to treat or improve symptoms of cardiovascular conditions including high blood pressure and heart failure.

ARBs commonly prescribed include:

- Azilsartan (Edarbi)
- Candesartan (Atacand)
- Eprosartan (Teveten)
- Irbesartan (Avapro)
- Losartan (Cozaar)

- Olmesartan (Benicar)
- Telmisartan (Micardis)
- Valsartan (Diovan)

Angiotensin Receptor - Neprilysin Inhibitors (ARNIs)
ARNIs are a drug combination of a neprilysin inhibitor and an ARB. Neprilysin is an enzyme that breaks down natural substances in the body that open narrowed arteries. By limiting the effect of neprilysin, it increases the effects of these substances and improves artery opening and blood flow, reduces salt (sodium) retention and decreases strain on the heart. This medication is usually prescribed for the treatment of heart failure.

ARNIs that are commonly prescribed include:

- Sacubitril/valsartan (Entresto)

Beta-blockers (also known as Beta-Adrenergic Blocking Agents)
Beta-blockers can make your heartbeat more slowly, with less force and lower your blood pressure and risk of a heart attack. You may sometimes be given a beta-blocker for arrhythmias (abnormal heart rhythms) or chest pain (angina). Beta-blockers block the action of adrenaline in your body. By doing this they reduce your blood pressure and heart rate. They have been shown to be a preventative against future heart attacks in people who have had a heart attack.

Beta-blockers that are commonly prescribed include:

- Acebutolol (Sectral)
- Atenolol (Tenormin)
- Betaxolol (Kerlone)
- Bisoprolol/hydrochlorothiazide (Ziac)
- Bisoprolol (Zebeta)
- Metoprolol (Lopressor, Toprol XL)
- Nadolol (Corgard)
- Propranolol (Inderal)

- Sotalol (Betapace)

Calcium Channel Blockers (also known as Calcium Antagonists or Calcium Blockers)
The medication interrupts the movement of calcium into the cells of the heart and blood vessels. It may decrease the heart's pumping strength and relax blood vessels. They are used to treat high blood pressure, chest pain (angina) caused by reduced blood supply to the heart muscle and some arrhythmias (abnormal heart rhythms).

Calcium channel blockers commonly prescribed include:

- Amlodipine (Norvasc)
- Diltiazem (Cardizem, Tiazac)
- Felodipine (Plendil)
- Nifedipine (Adalat, Procardia)
- Nimodipine (Nimotop)
- Nisoldipine (Sular)
- Verapamil (Calan, Verelan)

Cholesterol-lowering medicines
Various medications can lower blood cholesterol levels, but drugs other than statins are usually only used for patients in whom statins are not effective or who have serious side effects from statin therapy. They work in the body in different ways. Some affect the liver, some work in the intestines and some interrupt the formation of cholesterol from circulating in the blood. They are prescribed to lower LDL ('bad') cholesterol. Statins reduce your risk of heart attack and stroke by helping to lower your cholesterol. They also sometimes lower your triglycerides.

Statins together with a healthy low-fat diet will help lower your total cholesterol level and in particular your level of LDL 'bad' cholesterol. They also help stabilise the fatty plaques in your arteries. As cholesterol is produced overnight in your body this medicine will work best when taken at night. You must avoid grapefruit, grapefruit juice, pomegranate and pomegranate juice. Please talk to your medical practitioner about any potential risks as this can alter the level of statin which may be dangerous. You should report any symptoms of muscle pain, weakness or tenderness to your doctor as this can be a rare side effect of the medication and will need to be investigated if it occurs.

Statins help to stabilise plaque in arteries. They are often given to people after they have had a heart event (eg. heart attack, stroke or angina) – even if the person's cholesterol is in the 'normal' range. Your doctor may change the dose or type of statin you are taking, to make sure it is working properly and not causing side effects.

Cholesterol-lowering medications commonly prescribed include:

- Statins:
  - Atorvastatin (Lipitor)
  - Fluvastatin (Lescol)
  - Lovastatin (Mevacor)
  - Pitavastatin (Livalo)
  - Pravastatin (Pravachol)
  - Rosuvastatin (Crestor)
  - Simvastatin (Zocor)
- Nicotinic acids:
  - Niacin
- Cholesterol absorption inhibitor:
  - Ezetimibe (Zetia)
- Combination statin and cholesterol absorption inhibitors:
  - Ezetimibe/Simvastatin (Vytorin)

Vasodilators (anti-angina) medicines

Vasodilators are used to ease chest pain, to treat and prevent angina. It relaxes and widens your blood vessels and decreases your blood pressure.

A category of vasodilators called nitrates increases the supply of blood and oxygen to the heart while reducing its workload which can ease chest pain.

There are two types of nitrate medicines.

- Short-acting nitrate medicines relieve angina symptoms within a few minutes. These medicines are a spray or tablet that goes under your tongue (sublingual) and as a topical application (cream).

  The spray and tablets are absorbed through the lining of your mouth into your bloodstream. The most common short-acting nitrate medicine is glyceryl trinitrate (sometimes called 'GTN').
- Long-acting nitrate medicines prevent angina symptoms. They do not relieve an angina episode within a few minutes. These are usually a tablet that you swallow whole (you do not put them under your tongue like short-acting nitrate medicines). Nitrate medicines may also come as patches and you gradually absorb the medicine through your skin.

Nitrate Glyceryl Trinitrate (GTN)

Your GTN spray or tablet is a nitrate. Nitrates relax your coronary arteries and allow the blood to reach the heart muscle more easily. Always keep your GTN spray/tablet with you in your pocket or bag. Emergency GTN sprays are available from your pharmacist without a prescription. Always read the instructions and expiry dates.

Vasodilators commonly prescribed include:

- Isosorbide dinitrate (Isordil)
- Isosorbide mononitrate (Imdur)
- Hydralazine (Apresoline)
- Nitroglycerin (Nitro Bid, Nitro Stat)
- Minoxidil

Diuretics (water pills)

Diuretics cause the body to rid itself of excess fluids and sodium through urination. This helps to reduce your heart's workload. It also decreases the build-up of fluid in the lungs and other parts of the body, such as the ankles and legs. Different diuretics remove fluid at various rates and through different methods.
They are prescribed to help lower blood pressure. They are also used to help reduce swelling (oedema) from an excess build-up of fluid in the body.

Diuretics commonly prescribed include:

- Acetazolamide (Diamox)
- Amiloride (Midamor)
- Bumetanide (Bumex)
- Chlorothiazide (Diuril)
- Chlorthalidone (Hygroton)
- Furosemide (Lasix)
- Hydro-chlorothiazide (Esidrix, Hydrodiuril)
- Indapamide (Lozol)
- Metalozone (Zaroxolyn)
- Spironolactone (Aldactone)
- Torsemide (Demadex)

Other medicines

The information provided is not exhaustive. Your cardiologist or doctor may prescribe you other drugs.

These may be for a range of conditions such as high blood pressure or irregular heartbeats. If you have any concerns always discuss these with your medical practitioner.

Over the counter medicines

If you need to take any 'over the counter' medicines please discuss this with a pharmacist before you purchase them. Some of these drugs interact with your heart medicines.

Herbal remedies
This includes all remedies containing herbal preparations, which haven't been prescribed or recommended by your doctor, pharmacist or nurse. They may also be sold as 'herbal supplements' or 'herbal remedies'

Before taking any form of herbal medicine, you should talk to your doctor about whether it's safe to take it alongside any prescribed medications. In particular, you shouldn't take St. John's wort, as it can interact with a number of medicines prescribed for heart conditions.

Some herbal medicines may be taken in small amounts, but many are powerful substances that could affect how your prescribed treatment works.

Unlike prescribed medicines, not all herbal medicines have been rigorously tested, so, therefore, aren't licensed. Also, the strength of herbal medicines can vary from one manufacturer or brand to another.

"Wherever the art of medicine is loved, there is also a love of humanity."

Hippocrates

Medication Chart

Name of medication	Colour, shape and size?	What is it for?	Dose and frequency?	What times do you take it?	Date prescribed and any special instructions or notes?
Aspirin	Small white round tablet	Anti platelet to reduce clotting	75mg (1 tablet) once a day	At breakfast	18-11-2020 Take with food

DOWNLOAD: www.myheartandmind.co.uk/bookTBGO

Making Sense of Your Thoughts and Feelings

In 2016 and not for the first time, my life had become almost unrecognisable in a matter of 6 months. It all started with a freak accident. It was February and I was on a mission of wellbeing. It was in the middle of my regular martial arts class that I ruptured my Achilles tendon. It was during my recovery four weeks later that I had a Heart Attack. Then eight weeks after that, I had a diagnosis of breast cancer.

Initially, as I was discharged from the hospital, I felt elated. I thought that a few days rest and I would be back on 2 feet (well no not literally, I was in a non-weight bearing leg cast). I believed it was job done and I would be getting on with life.

That was not the case though and within hours of being back home, I crumpled. I wasn't expecting to feel so alone. I was mentally low, emotionally weak, so confused by medications, the lifestyle changes and the terminology that the cardiologists used. I was unmotivated and unsure of what I should eat or not eat and then there was the exercise too. I was anxious and frightened.

I was weak and breathless, the basic crawling up the stairs wasn't possible. I could only get so far then needed a rest. I felt fearful and had panic attacks, I was terrified I would have another event and again I wouldn't notice (It took me three days to see my doctor to get rid of my horrible indigestion!).

The physical feelings, the fatigue and yet sleeplessness was awful. I even seemed to have difficulty with brain fog. I would think of something to say, the word I wanted to use and yet a different word came out of my mouth. I felt uneasy, irritable and cross with myself, my life and the situation. I cried for no reason sometimes for a whole day.

I found life very bewildering, trying to get back to 'normal' and make changes to my lifestyle. What and how much exercise could I, should I do? How many tablets did I need to take, when and how was I going to remember? I had gone from just my HRT (hormone replacement therapy) pill to a full suite of them at various times of the day. Then there were the changes to my diet, managing my cholesterol and blood pressure and at the same time trying to reduce my stress levels. Life was an emotional roller coaster for me. Did I mention quitting smoking!

While I was thoroughly supported through my physical cardiac recovery. The rehab team were marvellous despite me being one of the 'difficult ones' with all my other health issues. But there was something missing, there was very little to help me with the emotional fallout and the practical side of implementing the changes needed to live my life well.

There is a happy ending though as I am lucky! My experience as a solution focussed therapist and life coach had given me the knowledge to recognise and understand what was happening to me. What I needed to do to be able to gain confidence, grow my knowledge and accept my thoughts and feelings. To live my life happy.

Recovery when living with a heart disease diagnosis isn't just about surviving; I want to help you thrive and feel good now. To take back control of your life, to help you to focus on all the things that you can do and worry less about what you can't. I want to empower you to be able to take responsibility for your life and your body. You can make all of the changes necessary and be happy and healthy.

I have chosen to become a warrior of the heart! I believe I'm lucky and my event is one of my many life experiences that I see as a great opportunity to focus on the things that really matter, to live and love life happy.

I want to help you gain the confidence to love the life you live. To have power over your thoughts, feelings and emotions. I want to support you through the changes to reduce your risk factors, I want you to understand your medication, your diagnosis, track your pain and manage your sleep. This will all help you have meaningful conversations with your medical team. You can live life happy after a cardiac event and when living with heart disease.

I am going to share with you some of the things that helped me get through those early roller-coaster days, although saying that I still use many of them now. As you read through this chapter and try out the various different ideas and techniques. I want you to remember that I believe that not everything works for all people and that some things work for some people.

To me, it's simple to understand why, we are all unique, different and distinct. Your view of the world, your life experiences, your thoughts and your beliefs are what make you, you. I really want you to throw yourself into having a go at everything though, you've nothing to lose and everything to gain. If it doesn't feel right and you really have given it a go, adapt it to suit your life or move on and try something else.

Feeling alone, thinking 'is it just me?'

As I mentioned I felt very isolated. I also had the added issue of not being able to attend Cardiac Rehab as I had my leg in a plaster cast and was non-weight bearing. This meant that I couldn't meet others that had had similar experiences or be reassured by the specialist cardiac team weekly. By chance when I was looking for reassurance on the British Heart Foundation website, I came across a forum thread that mentioned an online community on Facebook. I found and joined the British Hearties: Worldwide Hearties Survivors Support Group.

The members of this group literally saved my life. They were my lifeline as I was able to connect with other heart health survivors. As I began reading their posts it gave me comfort. I wasn't alone, others had been and were going through similar experiences. I gained knowledge, reassurance, I began to feel a little more 'normal' as I wasn't on my own and others experienced the same difficulties, emotions, thoughts and feelings as I did.

There are many friendly online groups available for particular and general heart conditions on Facebook. There is also the website Health Unlocked, it's currently the world's largest social network for health. Just use the search function, you can get pretty specific.

The purpose is to support each other, share heart-healthy tips, discuss news and information, ask questions and share experiences. You don't have to be active; you can just read and feel part of a community that understands. You may surprise yourself and help someone else and many people in the groups make good friends with each other.

You can of course join my group of hearties in the My Heart & Mind Community – it would be great to see you over on Facebook.

Trusting your heart and living life

While I was in hospital my lifestyle risks were assessed by the cardiac team. They gave me advice about changes I should make and how to look after myself when I left the hospital. I was so overwhelmed that I didn't really take much of what they said in. Luckily, I was given an information booklet and it included a plan for the first 4 weeks of my recovery at home. This is the first phase of cardiac rehabilitation. Follow the guidance given, it is full of great support and ideas. If you aren't given one then request a copy.

You should be given an appointment for cardiac rehabilitation. This is really valuable; it's a great opportunity to meet others, learn about how to reduce your risks and exercise your heart in a safe environment.

Make sure you ask to attend cardiac rehabilitation classes if they are available at your location. Cardiac rehabilitation involves exercise training (tailored to your personal needs). It helps you to begin to learn to trust your heart and your body. Your blood pressure is checked weekly and your heart rate is monitored throughout the exercise session. You'll learn to use the Borg Rating of Perceived Exertion (RPE) which is a way of measuring physical activity intensity level. You'll be given a plan for working at home too.

It's not just about physical health. Included in the weekly sessions are talks about emotional support and relaxation. Plus gain an understanding about making lifestyle changes to reduce your heart disease risk, such as eating a heart-healthy diet, maintaining a healthy weight and quitting smoking. Helping you to gain confidence and to trust your heart, mind and body again.

It's good to talk

Talk, talk, talk and then talk some more. This advice was given to me by a friend who had had a heart attack a number of years previously. At first, I found it difficult; for some reason, I felt embarrassed. I thought I would be judged like heart disease was an old person illness and that people would think it was my own fault. But I found that this was solid advice.

It lifted my spirits and I found it amazing how many people were interested and wanted me to talk about it. I found more people than I had imagined that had experienced a cardiac event themselves. I remember one time, in my early days when I wasn't feeling very confident about myself or life, I was getting a quote for some repairs to my sewing machine. Somehow it just came out in conversation. The kind gentleman I was talking to, took the time and shared his story with me, reassuring me, he made me feel understood, calm and in control.

Quiet that voice inside your head that says 'nobody cares' or 'no one is interested'. Pick up the phone, or talk face to face or online by Zoom or FaceTime. There's always someone that will listen, be honest and tell them you just need to talk about it. This is another reason to join an online community; there are so many groups, you don't have to just join one, you can become a member of as many as you are interested in. It's empowering to be able to ask for help and advice from people that have been where you are, don't be scared to admit your fears.

Be kind to yourself

Remember healing takes time. There is no quick fix; you don't get out of the hospital and then suddenly you're back on your feet.

It's a huge shock and a trauma. One moment all is okay in your world, the next minute you are very unwell and in a serious condition. Take it slowly inch by inch allowing yourself time to adjust, adapt and take the steps necessary to recover physically, mentally and emotionally.

Get plenty of rest, resting isn't laziness it's medicine. Sleep when you need, eat healthy foods, take your medications, ask for help when you need it and do as you are advised by your medical team.

Remember things will improve; the old saying 'time is a healer' is so true even if a little cliché.

Be in the now

Be in the present moment, in the now. The past has passed and the future has yet to happen. The present is a gift. You can't change what happened in the past and worrying about the future won't change it. Stay focused on the now and take each day as it comes. Live in each moment as it happens.

Learn meditation or find out about mindfulness. These are practices that will help you immensely. I use meditation daily for 10 minutes and during my recovery, I took an online mindfulness course. It was particularly useful for me to help me feel centred and I added in using affirmations about my heart healing, my health improving and that I am lucky.

The good stuff doesn't happen while you meditate. It's cumulative and will make a difference in keeping you calm, relaxed with a positive mindset throughout the day.

Accept current feelings and emotions

Become emotionally aware. Yes - you were physically repaired when you were sent home from the hospital. Yes - you have medications to keep you well and prevent any future problems. Yes - you have been given information about how to reduce your risks by making lifestyle changes as prevention.

But - it's the emotional side that can get us when we least expect it. I swung from happy to be alive, to wishing I hadn't survived - it was a shock to have these thoughts. I was anxious, cried for no apparent reason and felt angry.

These feelings are normal, they will pass and it may take a little time. Make sure you talk to friends, family and your medical team. You are not alone, ask for help as soon as you can. 'No person is an island'. It is not unusual to experience these thoughts, feelings and sensations, talk to your doctor, tell them how you are feeling, they can support you with medication, talking therapies and reassurance that this is not uncommon and it will pass. Again, this is where finding an online community can be helpful.

Friends and family

Spend time with people you love. Reach out to those that make you happy, that support you and love you.

Remember that some people just don't know what to say. They're scared of getting in touch with you in case they say the wrong thing. Make it easy for them. You need them to understand you. You also need to understand them.

If you have pets (or friends that will share theirs with you), spend some time stroking and caring for them. The therapeutic effect is well known, researchers at Washington State University have found that petting a dog or cat can relieve stress in just 10 minutes. Another study found that cat owners were 30 percent less likely to die of a heart attack or stroke than non-cat owners. Being loved and giving love is one of the best ways to heal yourself.

Don't confuse people who are always around you, with people who are always there for you. You will be pleasantly surprised at the people that become closer.

It is important to surround yourself with people that lift you up, people that are positive and encouraging. You'll notice the emotional vampires as you will be exhausted when you leave their company and, in some cases, while you are with them.

Don't worry if you feel let down by people that you thought were friends. I know it's easy for me to say as at the time you feel alone. You will find that other people that you didn't expect are there for you, be open and accepting, you'll find different friendships flourish.

Recovery time

Make the most of your recovery. Try to give yourself a structure for the day but allow yourself to do something that you haven't done before. How about binge-watching a television series that you've wanted to watch?

Maybe start reading a book? How about doing a jigsaw puzzle? Start something creative that you've never done before? Painting or drawing?

What about photography? Taking photos whilst you are out and building up your walking duration at the same time? You could listen to my podcast while you're out and about too.

Think about what you quite fancy doing. Perhaps you just haven't had the time. It doesn't have to be anything that you are good at, just something that gives you joy and pleasure.
I watched episodes of Chicago Fire back-to-back - not sure it did my heart any good with all the cliff-hangers and drama!

Find the treasure

Look for the positive in your recent experience. It was a shock, terrifying and no doubt life will never be the same, but that doesn't mean it can't be different or even better! I know my life is greatly improved and I am happier.

Spend time thinking about what you have been through and your recovery. Notice any differences in your life. There will be something good that has come out of this. You may not see it right now but keep looking and I am confident there will be something.

It won't be something you are expecting.

I no longer suffer fools gladly. I make the most of each and every day. I see my heart attack as a jolt to live my life consciously. It's reminded me to make a difference and change my life. I learnt that it's life's experiences and the people in my life that make me feel fulfilled.

Set goals for the day

I briefly mentioned earlier about keeping a structure to your day. After the first couple of weeks, once you are feeling stronger and feeling like you can do a little more each day. Start to set yourself goals; small, simple, achievable goals. Use a journal to capture them so you know what you have planned in mind. Don't go mad, if you just have one or two things to start with, you can increase in time. I really love keeping a paper list of what I want to get done. I tick each time I complete something, then at the end of the day I cross through them – it's very satisfying.

Start with small achievable and measurable goals. In the early days, it could be as simple as just going downstairs and making yourself a cup of tea. Gradually day by day make your goals slightly bigger. The information from the cardiac rehab team is a good starting place.

I couldn't walk and my heart was weak due to the time it took me to eventually get help. So, for me, it was spending 15 minutes to read and then action my emails. I found at first it was incredibly tiring but I felt a sense of accomplishment once I had finished. In time it built up until it was just a normal part of my day.

Feeling like you have a purpose

It's easy to lose that feeling of purpose when you have a heart disease diagnosis. You may find yourself focussing on what you can't do rather than on what you can. When you live your life with a sense of purpose, you begin living positively. It is important to start seeking out new opportunities and as you do, you'll start experiencing things that you feel will make a difference in your life and the lives of others.

Relationships are affected in a really good way when you live with purpose. You look for and create new friendships and relationships. It's easier to nurture your existing ones and build stronger connections with the people around you. With a purpose and meaning you tend to live life with more curiosity. It's easier to stay away from self-destructive habits such as smoking, drinking excessively and having a diet that isn't about good heart health. It helps you to seek out good ones that will help you create a difference in your world.

Look for purpose or meaning outside of yourself and your situation. Think about something that you can do to help or be of service to others.

Is there a charity that you could get involved with, maybe starting where you can volunteer from home? Making a donation isn't just about money. Your time and talent are just as valuable to all charities and non-profits.

Is there something that you can do that helps in your local community? Surround yourself with positive people, they will inspire you and encourage you. Maybe you can't change your family or work colleagues but outside of this, you have choice.

Is there something that you could contribute to? Such as writing an article for your local newsletter or newspaper? Helping out a neighbour or friend. Maybe in an online community by replying to someone who is in need. By helping others, you help them and yourself, to feel good.

Yes, it can be difficult to strike up conversations with strangers and you may feel awkward at first. But by talking to people, it can open your eyes to activities, causes or opportunities that you didn't know even existed.

Writing all about it

In keeping with the idea of talking and sharing your experience, one thing that helped me was to write about my cardiac journey. I just started a document on my laptop and kept adding to it, just a bit at a time. It felt good to write it out, it was therapeutic and cathartic, it helped me accept what I had been through.

Another useful idea is to keep a day-by-day journal or diary. The entries don't need to be very long or detailed, just enough to keep you aware of how you are feeling and what you are doing. You can look back through the pages when you're feeling frustrated or sad. You'll be able to see you are improving day by day.

For some people it may be slower and subtle changes, remember I couldn't walk due to being in a plaster cast so my exercise wasn't great but it did highlight other changes and differences, such as being able to use a wheelchair around my home as I wasn't allowed to use crutches. Seeing my progress was an important part of my recovery.

You can write about what you've achieved, how you are feeling, things to do or where your pain/energy/fatigue level is on a 1-10 scale. You can capture your thoughts about the things that you want to discuss with your medical team or cardiac specialists. You can even start a bucket list of all the things you want to do in the future.

Keeping a journal helps you stay focused and moving forwards. It doesn't have to be very long, just enough to keep you aware of how you are improving daily. I journalled every evening, I'd reflect over the day and list of 5 positive things that had happened/or that I was grateful for on the day. I'd think about the small stuff, the sun shining, a smile from a stranger or my phone.

Journaling for Emotional Wellbeing

The why
I really struggled with life and my thoughts after my heart attack. That was until something life-changing happened. It caused me to change my thinking as I realised two things. Firstly, that 'I was lucky' and secondly, 'that how I felt was up to me'.

It was my life, my thoughts, my feelings and my actions so that meant I had control over how I was feeling. I had to stop waiting for something or someone to make things better. Only I had the power to change them and therefore my life.

I decided that I would start with six basic simple activities. I would do them throughout the day. Doing them would give me some structure to my day and that was what I needed too. They were the easy things that I knew would improve my emotional wellness and motivate me to make the lifestyle changes I needed to make.

You can keep the pages and go back to them to review how you've been feeling. It's a great way of noticing what you have done and gain an understanding of your journey so far. It can also help you plan for the future, the things and ideas you have for your bucket list. Alternatively, you can dispose of them in any way you see fit, it's the doing that counts for making a change in how we feel and what we achieve.

The what

Keeping a journal or a diary helps you stay focused and moving forwards. It doesn't have to be very long, just enough to keep you aware of how you are improving daily.

By doing these six simple activities regularly (daily is best) it will help you become your best self, adopt a positive outlook on life, practice gratitude and reflect on your growth one day at a time.

You can write about what you have achieved, how you are feeling and rate yourself on a scale of 1 -10. You can use it to capture your thoughts and feelings. All the things that you might want to discuss with the important people in your life.

You could even use it to start a bucket list of all the things you want to do in the future.

The how

Starting with a blank sheet of paper can be daunting, where do I start was always the thought I had when I tried to keep a diary earlier in my life. I always allowed my thoughts to get in my way.

Now that I know the value of journaling (I didn't for a very long time), I made a decision to just go do it! I don't think about it, don't allow thoughts to come to mind like 'I will do it later' or 'it's not important'. I just decide it's time to start and now it's your turn to make a difference in your life.

To help with the blank page problem and share with you the exercises I did, you will find a template for you to complete at the end of this chapter.

Completing your journal

Now

Simply write today's date, hush your mind of thoughts about the past or the future. Take a couple of slow deep breaths and just focus on right this moment. What word springs to mind, add one word that describes this moment and how you would like the day to be or how you would like to feel.

Purpose

During recovery, it can feel like you are just existing. Bring purpose into your day. What one thing are you going to achieve today? It doesn't matter how small it is but it is something you want to do for yourself. Decide that no matter what, you are going to do it and you are doing it today.

You could choose more than one thing but start small, with baby steps, look forward to achieving that 'thing' and ticking it off when it's completed.

Belief

You may or may not confess to talking to yourself? I know I do. It's those thoughts that go around in your mind that can affect your mood, your ability and what your unconscious mind thinks is important to you.

When we speak in 'affirmations' our unconscious mind hears the affirmation as a fact that is yet to be and it immediately seeks ways in which to manifest this new fact. Yes, your unconscious is taking your affirmation in as fact. Our unconscious mind doesn't know the difference between reality and our imagination. An example of this is when you are engrossed watching a movie or reading a book. You really feel the emotions of the characters on the screen. Its why horror films can scare us, it's not real but our imagination triggers the chemicals and hormones within our bodies. Have you ever been on the edge of your seat ready to fight or flight?

So, let's re-programme our mind using repetition and empowering phrases. Each day choose a positive affirmation, write it in your journal as a reminder. Then commit to saying it three to five times to yourself a number of times throughout the day.

It can be out loud or in your head. You could leave post-it notes around your home or office to remind you, you could decide to repeat them every time you walk through a doorway or you could set an alarm on your phone or ask Alexa to remind you. You could sing them in the shower or say them to yourself while you are cleaning your teeth. Make sure, they are positive.

Journaling

Find say ten minutes to sit with your journal and freely express how you feel and what you think right now. No censorship, no one is going to read it unless you want them to.

If you don't know what to write, just write I don't know what to write and just see what happens. Commit to giving yourself just this time to really say to no one in particular what's going on for you. What you think, feel and experience, what you want etc.

Future

What do you want to do in the future? What are your goals, dreams and your ambitions? Add anything that you would like to experience, be, have, do, see or hear. There's nothing too big or anything too small. Just capture your hopes, wishes and ambitions. Begin a list of what you want to do, so often you see something or hear of something that excites you but within a few moments, days if you are lucky, you have forgotten.

Gratitude

Sometimes you can forget how lucky you are to have what you do. It's like the choice I could have made about my heart attack. Am I the victim of genetics and life choices and my life is now over? Or am I grateful that I am alive, lucky that I had ruptured my Achilles tendon and was therefore on blood thinners while I had my heart attack? I may not have made it.

At some point during the day make a list of five positive things that have happened or that you are grateful for in the last 24 hours. Remember that sometimes it is the little things that bring the most pleasure. Things that you are happy about, the stuff that gave you a smile or felt good. Sometimes it will be something small like the sun shone or that you're grateful for your mobile phone. At other times it might be a huge thing like completing a course or like me just being able to walk for half an hour.

Try not to repeat yourself though, look for all the little things that make you pleased or fortunate; a free refill of coffee or someone smiled at you.

Achievement

Today has been a good day because?

At the end of the day as you are beginning to think about time for sleep take a few moments to reflect on your day and your life. Write three things that you have completed today. Big or small they all count. It could be 15 minutes of managing your emails, maybe choosing to have some fruit instead of cake, taking the stairs instead of the lift, or filling up the windscreen washer in your car. Become aware of what you have done today.

Your journal options

To leave it as it is, put it away for tomorrow and get on with your day. Use it just as an outlet, a brain dump, for goal setting and even ranting.

You can go back later to review your words, or not; you can destroy it without re-reading. Although my suggestion is that if you are going to review your journaling, it is best to leave it for around 5-6 weeks before you do.

Alternatively, you can review your words when you've finished. If they aren't helpful, kind or useful, consider what you can change to make you feel good now? If you wouldn't say them to a friend, why would you say them to yourself? Noticing how we speak to ourselves can be really empowering especially when we use positive affirmations to change our beliefs about ourselves and our situations.

"We must be willing to let go of the life we've planned, so as to have the life that is waiting for us."

Joseph Campbell

Emotional Wellbeing Journal

NOW today is:

PURPOSE today I will achieve?

BELIEF today's affirmation is?

GRATITUDE today's great because?

JOURNALING about today?

ACHIEVEMENT today I did?

FUTURE to do, see, be, have or hear?

DOWNLOAD: www.myheartandmind.co.uk/bookTBGO

Easing Anxiety, Panic & Fear

Is anxiety good or bad? A little bit of anxiety can be helpful as it motivates you to do something and get things done. Too much anxiety can cause many physical and emotional problems, it is not good for your health.

Stress is one of your risk factors and it can be difficult to realise how you can reduce it.

When you're feeling anxious, your body releases stress hormones, such as adrenaline and cortisol. They are part of our survival instinct; the fight or flight response.

These hormones cause the symptoms of anxiety, such as an increased heart rate, palpitations and increased sweating. When your body is continually being flooded with these hormones you can feel unable to concentrate, quite irritable and tearful, feel on edge, not be able to relax and have difficulties sleeping.

After a cardiac event or a diagnosis of heart disease, it can be a worrying and stressful time.

On the next few pages, you'll find some ideas about how to tame those butterflies that feel like a herd of elephants in your tummy.

Each exercise should take around ten minutes to change how you feel. So, you can see and think clearly.

Breathe deeply to release anxiety

- Take a three-minute break. When you notice you're feeling anxious, panicked or uptight, STOP and go somewhere safe.
- Take a breath in through your nose slowly and deeply to the count of six.
- Imagine breathing in peace and calm.
- Hold for the count of two or three as you take a moment.
- Then exhale through your mouth to the count of six or longer if it is comfortable.
- Allow yourself to imagine feeling all and any of that tension and anxiety flowing out of you as you let the breath go.

It's best to repeat this breathing technique nine times. Quietening your breath, your thoughts and allowing your body to settle.

Follow your breath as it flows in and out. Do not try to control it. This is a good way to relax in the midst of any activity. It allows you to find a breathing pattern that is natural and relaxing for you. The counts are just a guide. Ideally, the out-breath should be longer than your inhale.

Mind-body connection

Science has proven that how we arrange our bodies affects how we feel about ourselves.

This idea will only take 30 to 60 seconds and can be completed anywhere and even if it was in public no one would be particularly aware other than how much more relaxed you seemed.

When we sit up straight, we are more likely to remember positive memories or think of something positive. The way we stand, sit and walk, actually affects our mood and happiness.

To create the change in how you feel by moving your body in simple. You'll need about a minute to follow these simple and easy steps.

- Take a breath in deeply
- Exhale slowly and gently all the way out
- Drop your shoulders down
- Lift your chin up
- Release your jaw
- Stand or sit tall
- And breathe in and sigh as you let go

Reduce stimulants

Make the decision to avoid caffeine, alcohol, fizzy sweet drinks and large amounts of sugary sweets. You may believe the extra rush from a cup of coffee, a glass of alcohol or a helping of cake will make you feel better and give you more energy.

It's short-lived; after the initial hit it's all downhill and they can also aggravate the symptoms of anxiety due to the effects they have on the nervous system. The same applies to nicotine. Coffee and booze will affect your sleep so limit or stop until you're feeling better.

I appreciate that it isn't as easy as it sounds, remember that it takes only 42 days to create a new habit, that's less than 2 months. Reward yourself every time you make the right choice and let it go when you don't. It's not the end of the world, just a decision made and that moment in time.

Who do you think you are talking to?
What is your inner voice saying? What are you saying or thinking to yourself? If you wouldn't say it to a friend, don't say it to yourself. If it is less than useful, has any negative impact and makes you feel unhappy. Tell yourself to 'shut the hell up'.

Focus on positive thoughts, find something that is more useful and helpful to say to yourself. Change self-talk to useful phrases such as 'I can handle this' and 'what can I do next'?

Whilst again this only takes a minute to actually do. It can take a while to recognise when you are doing it and what you are saying that is making you anxious. Becoming aware that when you're not feeling good, it's usually because of what you are saying or thinking to yourself. That you can listen to the story you have been telling yourself and change it to something empowering and uplifting.

Aromatherapy
The origin of lavender goes back some 2,500 years in history; it is one of the most versatile essential oils. It may be useful for treating anxiety, insomnia, depression and restlessness.

It is physically and emotionally calming, relaxing and balancing. You don't necessarily need to have a massage with essential oils to create calm and relaxation, therefore reducing stress and anxiety.

You can burn incense or candles. Sprinkle a few drops of oil on a cushion/pillow or use a hot stone or oil burner.

For an immediate calming effect rub a drop of the oil into your cupped hands. Inhale deeply drawing the scent into your amygdala (the emotional warehouse) to calm your mind and body.

Jump around

I mentioned the mind-body connection earlier. This is another example of how you can use your body to alleviate feelings of pressure, fear, anxiety and worry. Remember you have a body and it was made for moving around. Get your personal energy flowing and moving around your being.

If you are caught up in anxious thoughts stand up and move around. Shake yourself out of it. Wave your arms around, skip or hop, jump up and down. Literally, in less than four minutes, you will be feeling differently.

Taking some exercise and raising your heart rate a little releases natural endorphin (your very own feel-good chemicals). Okay so going to the gym will take more than 10 minutes. But why not go briskly up and down the stairs a couple of times. Go for a paced walk or put on some upbeat music and dance it out?

Time to unwind

This is an activity that is going to use your imagination and tune in to your bodily sensations. It should take you less than five minutes. I would recommend you read through the process first a couple of times so you can commit to memory the steps. It is okay to stop and refer to this page though, remember it is whatever works for you. You could even record the instructions on your smartphone and play them back to yourself. Remember to leave enough space so you can do the work. Remember there is no right or wrong way as we are all unique.

Like at the start of most activities I want you to take a long slow deep breath in and then out. Take moment to be in the moment. Now, you can close your eyes if you wish to as sometimes for some people it is easier to visualise this way.

Begin to become aware of that anxiety as a feeling in a part of the body (maybe in the tummy, chest, head or mouth). Where do you feel that anxiety, how do you know you are anxious? I seem to find mine more often than not as a sensation at the pit of my stomach. But it really does differ from person to person and situation to situation as sometimes it can be tension in my jaw.

Once you've located where that sensation is. Start to visualise in your mind's eye pushing the sensation out of the body as a shape. You may be able to see the imaginary shape or maybe you will just sense it, hanging there in space outside of you. For some it might be that you hear the anxiety, push that sounds outside of yourself.

What shape is it? Is it jagged or sharp cornered? This is your chance to change the shape to something more comforting, perhaps cloud-like. If it is a sound, is it scratchy or flat in pitch? If so, change it in your imagination to something soothing and melodious.

Can you imagine what colour the shape is? You can now visualise changing the colour. Make the shape the colour that represents soothing and calm. If it's auditory, if it's loud imagine turning it down, maybe there is hiss or crackle ease that sound to be comforting.

Visualise or sense that your representation (image or sound) is spinning and turning in front of you. Pay attention to the direction of the movement of the image or how the sound is resonating.

Now imagine taking control of the representation and changing the direction of the spin so it's spinning the opposite way, in the other direction. This applies to the resonance and direction of sounds too.

Then gently and carefully begin pulling the revolving representation back inside you. Continuing to allow the spinning and the feeling to move in the opposite/different direction, slowing down and unwinding.

And as you do, you begin to notice how that feeling is moving down and changing as you feel even more relaxed now.

Affirmations/Incantations

When I mentioned beliefs earlier, I talked about using affirmations. But what are affirmations? Affirmations are a statement made about the future in the present tense as if it had already happened in the past.

The idea is to create new neural pathways of thought so that we move to think more favourably about ourselves, our lives and our future. We do this by practicing the thoughts and phrases and like everything I talk about, it's one thing to know about it but it is only when you do it that it makes a difference to your life.

One thing to note is that your unconscious mind can't be easily fooled so you may have to move a little slowly. For instance, if you are going to a job interview you are likely to be anxious and nervous so if you use the affirmation 'I am calm and relaxed' your unconscious mind will reject it. In this instance, it may be better to start with something like 'I can relax and feel calm' or 'I have prepared and am ready'.

Affirmations work best when you recite each of your affirmations as many times as possible. Repeat your affirmations throughout the day.

You might want to put notes around your home to remind you. Perhaps you'll create the habit of saying them while brushing your teeth, or walking, driving or you use them as part of a meditation. Such a simple thing to do, isn't it? It can completely

change how we feel, as it helps create the new habit of saying things that are positive and empowering. Allowing us to feel and think thoughts that create a life living happy.
Try some of these, adapt and change them to suit what feels good and right for you.

- I am happy, content and so relaxed
- I am in total control of my thoughts
- I am really confident every day
- I am calm and relaxed at all times
- I choose to think positively about myself
- I accept myself unconditionally
- I am happy to be alive!

Meditate
When you meditate, you relax and this means your stress levels fall significantly and your body begins to calm and normalise, including your blood pressure.

The soothing qualities of the meditative state bring peace to the mind, body and nervous system. You are then able to break through the hyperactivity in your aroused imbalanced autonomic nervous system and as a result your nervous system is able to reset itself.

Not meditated before? Here's a quick and simple way to start, give this a try:

- Set a timer for 10 or more minutes. I use my iPhone with some relaxing music playing and set it to turn the music off after 10 minutes; gentler than an alarm going off.
- Get comfortable in a chair and relax. Preferably not laying down as this might encourage you to doze off, so you might

want to use this at night if you have difficulty sleeping too.

- Place your feet flat on the floor; hands loosely on your lap.
- Use slow and gentle deep breathing for two or three breaths finding your own rhythm. Close your eyes, concentrate your focus on your breathing for a few breaths.
- In your imagination take yourself to your favourite place, somewhere you enjoy and feel safe. Maybe a beach, woodlands, a park, in the country or even in town.
- Imagine all the little details, what you would see, hear, smell and feel.
- And as you begin to become more relaxed start saying the word 'one' over and over gently in your mind.
- And I don't know exactly how your mind wanders off, gently, notice it, accepting that it is okay and then bring your thoughts back to the word 'one' and continue repeating it slowly and calmly to yourself.
- When the music stops or your alarm goes off, job done and continue with your day.

Guided Relaxation

Guided relaxation is similar to meditation. The difference is that rather than practising it yourself you are guided on a journey.

Give it a go, you may be surprised at how relaxed your feel. You can listen to my free audio download 'Washing It Away'

I will take you on a journey of guided relaxation for 20 minutes. You will get access to a twenty-minute break to drift off and relax, take time out for yourself and let any tension float away.

Get yourself comfortable in a chair at a time when you won't be disturbed.

bedroom your personal sanctuary used only for sleep and good sex!

Get organised

Sometimes it can be thoughts about the next day that can keep you awake.

Make sure you have everything prepared and organised. Take a few moments the evening before to review your plans for the next day. Work out what you will need and write a list of what you want to achieve. You can then retire to your bed knowing that everything is ready and that you need not concern yourself with anything. Remember the little things that can be taken for granted.

Background sounds

One reason why you might wake in the night could be because of sounds from the building or from outside waken you. Having background soothing sounds that gradually rise and fall in volume can prevent the noises startling you while asleep.

Rainfall, ocean waves, sounds from nature and the low rumble of a distant thunder storm are known to put a person to sleep. There are plenty available on the internet for you to download. My daughter's preference is heavy rainfall. Give them all a try and find out what soothes you the most.

Your routine

With children, it is well known that routine is key to good sleep hygiene. As adults, we seem to have forgotten this. Just like children, our bodies need habits and patterns.

Getting up at the same time every day and having a standardised bedtime helps create a regular body clock that means you're less tired waking up and more likely to sleep well at night.

It is recommended that you should give yourself an hour before you go to bed to unwind and relax.

It may be having a long bath or reading a book but whatever it is do it regularly. After a while, it will become a habit and will signal your body that it is time for sleep.

Valerian

I first came across valerian when I started menopause. It was suggested by my doctor. I found it very effective for helping me go to sleep, stay asleep and sleep longer.

Valerian is a herb and is classed as a supplement. There isn't enough research and studies at present to be definitive about how effective it is and how much is the optimum dose. So, this is something that you might want to try out for yourself. Always check with your doctor, pharmacist or herbalist especially if you take other medication.

Note: It does have an unpleasant smell to me but one of my cats absolutely adores it, even more than catnip!

As always check with your pharmacist before taking any over the counter medication or herbal remedies. This includes valerian, as there may be interactions with your current prescription.

Reduce caffeine

Whilst you may be using caffeine to keep you awake during the day it can be affecting how well you sleep.

Make the change to decaffeinated coffee, tea and fizzy drinks. If you quit completely, you may find you have a headache for a couple of days but this will soon pass.

If you find it difficult to cut caffeine out of your diet completely then do reduce your consumption. Only having drinks with caffeine in the morning.

Stay clear of caffeine tablets and read the packets of pain killers as some of them contain caffeine to enhance the effect of pain relief.

Essential oils that help sleep
Try lavender and chamomile.

Chamomile especially as a drink or in oil form is one of the best herbs for reducing stress and promoting relaxation and sleep. The tea can be found in many supermarkets.

Lavender oil is another that is well known to aid sleep and relaxation. You can put a few drops on a pillow or in an oil burner.

Try having a cup of chamomile tea and a warm bath about 1 hr before bed. Take about 20 drops of diluted lavender oil, rub it over your body and get into a bath with Epsom salts (they contain magnesium that helps with sleep too). Relax for about 20 minutes then continue with the rest of your routine.

Worrying
Sometimes the cause of insomnia can be because you are worrying about poor sleep.

Do you tell yourself that you won't sleep? Do you find yourself telling others that you won't sleep? Do you lay in bed worrying about not being able to sleep the moment you're in bed?

If this is the case it can be your belief about the lack of sleep that is the problem and keeping you awake.

Change it up. Begin by noticing what you are saying. Practice changing your thoughts and tell yourself you can sleep and will sleep easily and effortlessly. You'll be surprised at how this simple thing can make a huge difference.

Talk yourself to sleep

Yes, surprisingly there are many ways to talk yourself to sleep this includes the old faithful counting sheep.

If sheep are a bit old school for you then here is another idea that can work for you.

Use the alphabet

Get yourself comfortable in bed, close your eyes and take a few slow deep relaxing breaths.

- Decide on a theme and begin at A.
- List all of the items in your theme that start with each letter of the alphabet consecutively.
- If you get to the end of the alphabet start again but do it backwards from Z to A

Here are some suggested themes:

Fruits, vegetables, animals, product names, girls or boys names, makes of cars, trees or the periodic table etc.

Future visualisations

When you're in bed and comfortable, run through your next day (or a future event) in your mind. Take it moment by moment and be aware of the detail, the colours, the sounds, the feelings and any smells or tastes that you might experience.

Imagine everything going wonderfully, just the way you'd want it to. All is well.

Nap successfully

If you do need to take a nap it is helpful to follow this advice as sleeping during the day uses up your sleep drive.

- Keep it to between 20-30 minutes or less.
- Keep it short and sweet, using a timer is a good idea.
- The earlier in the day the better, no later than 2-3 pm.

Know your sleep goal?
When making a change I think it best to start with the end in mind. It's helpful to know what you want to achieve so you can recognise when you get there and celebrate.

Take a few moments to decide on your sleep goal, what you want to achieve, what to you feels like a good sleeping habit.

Here are some questions that might help you focus positively on what you do want.

- What time do you want to go to bed?
- What time do you want to get up?
- How long to fall asleep?
- How many hours asleep?
- How long to go back to sleep?
- To nap or not to nap? If so, how many and for how long?
- What are you going to do to help you keep your sleep goal?
- What do you see being the biggest roadblocks to being able to hit your goal?
- What help from others do you need?
- What will help you to achieve your sleep goal?
- How will you notice your success and how will you celebrate your small wins?
- What changes do you think you might make?

Keep a sleep journal

You can look for patterns. Make changes to habits. Have a record that you can discuss with your medical practitioners.

It will also help you identify and keep a record of how much or little sleep you actually had. Sometimes we do sleep but we feel like we haven't and when you're tired it is easy to lose track and feel like you never get any sleep.

I would recommend keeping a sleep diary as soon as you begin to recognise a problem and complete it over at least a two-week period.

As I have said before you are the most important person in any intervention. By keeping records, it can help you communicate effectively with your doctor. If you need to see a doctor or healthcare professional about your sleep issues you will have evidence of your sleep-wake pattern which can help with a diagnosis and treatment.

Journaling for Sleep

Prior to my heart attack, I used to sleep like a baby. Maybe I liked to hit the snooze button in the morning, a bit too often than was good for me but sleep hadn't been an issue since I was a teenager.

After a life-changing event, particularly a cardiac event or a diagnosis of heart disease there are lots of things that can impact your sleep pattern and quality.

Sleeping poorly is exhausting

My heart attack started while I was asleep. It literally woke me up with an upset stomach and feeling sweaty, leaving me with indigestion that I ignored! This was something that impacted my thoughts as I was nervous about falling asleep and not waking if it happened again. When I did get to sleep, I was waking at silly o'clock in the morning and couldn't get back to sleep. And .... I haven't mentioned my waking in the night to deal with my sweat-drenched bedclothes caused by having my HRT (hormone replacement therapy) stopped suddenly. I was so tired and exhausted that I was napping throughout the day.

If you're having difficulty sleeping, it can become a vicious circle. The more you lay in bed worrying about not sleeping the less likely you are to go to sleep.

The first step in making changes is to begin by identifying the cause or causes. These can be many and varied from your environment, your behaviour, your diet and how you think. For example, drinking too much caffeine before bedtime, not exercising or poor sleep hygiene.

If it is not obvious and you can't understand why you're not sleeping, keeping a sleep journal can help. The journal will help to pinpoint if you're consistently waking at a similar time, what you've done that day, what you've eaten etc., to see if there is any pattern.

How to use your sleep journal
On the following pages, you'll find a two-part sleep journal.

The first part can be completed throughout the day but at the end of the day before you go to sleep is good too. It helps to capture your daytime activities and your sleep ritual both of which can influence how well you sleep.

The second part of the journal is about your sleeping and ability to go back to sleep. This is to be completed upon waking each morning. You're not expected to stay awake. It is not meant to keep you awake either. Just make a note the next morning of your sleep pattern. None of this journaling is an exact science. A guesstimate is fine, a rough guess about what you believe to be the times you woke and the length of time you were awake.

Your journaling will include asking you some of the following questions to help you identify possible causes and things that could be changed to help improve your sleep quality.

What did you eat and when?
This will help you identify types of foods, the amount of food and the time that you are eating. All of these may have an impact on your sleep.

You are asked about how much exercise did you do?
At what time and when during the day? If you don't take any exercise then this is likely to be a potential impact on your sleep just as the timing of doing high impact exercise.

Do you nap?
Did you know we have a sleep drive? If we nap too often, too long or at the wrong time this can interfere with our sleep at night.

How do you feel?
Happy, sad, anxious etc and why? Often it can be our thoughts that keep us awake like my fear of sleeping through another heart attack. There are lots of techniques that can help quieten those racing, worrying thoughts.

Many if not all of us take medications.
By identifying when and what you take along with what time you take it can often start an interesting conversation with your pharmacist. In some instances, some medications can make you sleepy and tired. When I first started taking beta-blockers, I noticed I was ready to nap within 30 minutes, if I sat still, I would nod off. It's not the case now as I have got used to the effect but it's worth talking to your doctor if you think there may be a connection.

The journal asks you about your bedtime routine.
How much time you spend in bed not asleep? Both of these areas can be important to review as they are behavioural. They can be changed quite easily once you know what it is that you are doing. You can try simple changes and see if they make the difference you need.

And the journal asks about what you try to help you sleep.
Do you use meditation, mindfulness or other relaxation techniques? If you do, you can isolate which ones make the most difference for you and start to use them regularly.

Sleep Journal (part 1)

Daytime activities and sleep ritual - complete each night before going to bed

	Monday	Tuesday	Wednesday	Thursday	Friday	Saturday	Sunday
What did you eat and when?							
Did you exercise? What? When? How long?							
Did you nap? When? Where? How long?							
Alcohol or caffeine? What? When? Amount?							
How did you feel? Happy, sad, anxious, angry etc. and why?							
Medicines? What, when & how much?							
What was your bedtime routine?							
Did you use meditation or relaxation techniques?							
What time did you go to bed?							

DOWNLOAD: www.myheartandmind.co.uk/bookTBGO

Sleep Journal (part 2)

Sleeping and going back to sleep – complete upon waking each morning

	Monday	Tuesday	Wednesday	Thursday	Friday	Saturday	Sunday
What time did you wake up?							
Time spent in bed not asleep. What did you do?							
Sleep breaks. Did you wake up/get up during the night? If so, what did you do?							
Quality of sleep and any other comments.							
How many hours did you sleep?							

DOWNLOAD: www.myheartandmind.co.uk/bookTBGO

Sleep Tips and Tricks

As I mentioned it is really helpful to know what you want to achieve, this gives you direction. However, there is a caveat to this. It's that once you've decided on what success will look like for you, you start to focus on the doing, the action taking. Avoid obsessing over the actual goal, about how far away it seems or how long it might take. Stay in the moment and take things day by day. It is important to notice the small differences and see your progress, it's as much about the journey as the destination.

How to use your sleep checklist

Included in the following pages is my checklist of ideas to help you improve your sleep. They address a number of different areas as I explained earlier. These include your bedroom, your habits before you go to bed, what you can do to help your body along with tips to help quiet your mind and thoughts.

The list is not exhaustive by any means, there are many more ideas that can help. Do start by reviewing your sleep journal and take note of behaviours and habits that aren't helpful for a good night's sleep.

Take a look at the checklist and mark the ones that you think apply to you and your lifestyle. The ones that you think will make a difference to your sleep quality if you make the changes.

Remember not to try everything at once as you won't know what worked and what didn't. Also, note that that some things take repetition or practice. A new habit takes around 42 days to create, although sometimes much quicker.

Sleep checklist

Behaviours and environment that effect your sleep

- ☐ Your bedroom should be cool – between 60 and 67 degrees
- ☐ Your bedroom should also be free from any noise that can disturb your sleep
- ☐ Your bedroom should be free from any light
- ☐ Check your room for noises or other distractions
- ☐ Does your bed partner disturb you such as tossing and turning or snoring?
- ☐ Are there 'white noise' machines such as computers, humidifiers, fans and other devices?
- ☐ Consider blackout curtains
- ☐ Consider using eye shades
- ☐ Consider using ear plugs
- ☐ Make sure your mattress is comfortable and supportive. The one you have been using for years may have exceeded its life expectancy
- ☐ Have comfortable pillows
- ☐ Make the room attractive and inviting for sleep
- ☐ Ensure it is free of allergens that might affect you
- ☐ There are no objects that might cause you to slip or fall if you have to get up

- ☐ Avoid naps, especially in the afternoon
- ☐ Don't watch TV, Netflix on your laptop/tablet or have office equipment in your bedroom
- ☐ Your bedroom should be your sanctuary, your place for sleep or sex!!
- ☐ If you have a TV or other tech in your bedroom you may be tempted to use them
- ☐ Make sure you avoid using technology 30-60 minutes before going to bed
- ☐ Do you have to use your mobile phone as an alarm clock?
- ☐ If your phone is by your bed make sure the alerts are off, the volume is off and it is facedown beside the bed
- ☐ Make sure you have everything organised and ready for the next day
- ☐ Before bed, have a warm bath with a few drops of lavender oil or a shower with lavender scented body wash
- ☐ Run through the next day in your mind, imagine everything going wonderfully well, just the way you'd want it to be
- ☐ Get yourself a special notebook and a pen that you like to write with. If your thoughts require it write down any actions or ideas for the next day
- ☐ Do you find you worry when lying in bed? Allow yourself 10 minutes 'worry time' early in the evening, well before your bedtime

Using your mind to help you sleep

- ☐ Breathing exercises, one of the quickest ways to lower stress and relax is to breathe deeply
- ☐ Check your belief, are you really deprived of sleep? We often think we are sleeping less than we actually do. Use a sleep journal or a sleep tracking app on your phone to measure the

amount of sleep you do get. If you are getting 7-8 hours' sleep you can change this belief you hold about not getting enough sleep.

- ☐ Do be aware that if you use your mobile device the blue light and notifications can be disruptive to sleep
- ☐ Do you prefer rain, ocean waves, sounds from nature or the low rumble of a distant thunder storm? There are plenty of background sounds that are known to help sleep available to download on the internet
- ☐ Do you tell yourself that you won't sleep? If this is the case it can be your belief about the lack of sleep that is keeping you awake. Change this thought and say to yourself 'I will sleep easily and effortlessly'
- ☐ Learn to meditate
- ☐ Listen to soft music with a slower beat than your heart. Something that's easy on the ear and relaxing
- ☐ Make yourself some affirmations and repeat them. It is a positive statement made about the future but in the present tense, as if it had already happened in the past. After a while of repetition, you may surprise yourself and be asleep
- ☐ Practice progressive muscle relaxation
- ☐ Practice self-soothing during the day. Noticing when you are becoming stressed and saying to yourself 'Stop, relax, soften'
- ☐ Talk yourself to sleep. Start at the beginning of the alphabet and find things that start with each letter consecutively. If you get to the end of the alphabet start doing it backwards from Z to A
- ☐ Use a guided relaxation recording
- ☐ Visit a hypnotherapist
- ☐ Visualise a future event. When in bed and comfortable, run through something you are looking forward to in the future.

Imagine everything going wonderfully, just the way you'd want it to

Helping your body help you sleep

- ☐ Are you active? Regular cardio exercise is the best, but even light exercise such as stretching is beneficial in aiding sleep
- ☐ Avoid alcohol as although alcohol can make you sleepy it is actually a stimulant and a diuretic
- ☐ Eat foods containing tryptophan eaten with carbohydrates. These include chicken breast, turkey, tuna, soya beans and salmon
- ☐ Herbal remedies such as valerian, passionflower, hops, lavender, lemon balm and Jamaican dogwood. If you are taking any prescribed medicines always check with your medical practitioner first
- ☐ Include more thiamine (vitamin B1) and magnesium in your diet. Good sources of these are whole grains, nuts and green leafy veggies
- ☐ Keep a sleep journal
- ☐ Make an appointment to see your medical practitioner
- ☐ Make sure you drink plenty of water throughout the day. It's a fine balance though as too much will have you up in the night to use the loo
- ☐ Melatonin is a naturally occurring hormone that your body produces at night. It's what helps regulate your sleep-wake cycle and like other supplements it is available over the counter.
- ☐ Only eat a light meal in the evening, make it something easy to digest
- ☐ Over-the-counter remedies; these are available in supermarkets, online and at a chemist. As with herbal remedies always check with your doctor as they may interact

with other medication you are taking

- ☐ Prescribed sleep medications can provide temporary relief but it's important to understand that they aren't a cure for insomnia. It's best to use them as a last resort and only on an as-needed basis
- ☐ Reduce caffeine, tea, coffee, green tea and fizzy drinks, look out for painkillers containing caffeine too
- ☐ Reduce your intake of sugar
- ☐ Stop adding salt to your food before trying it first, you may find you don't need it or as much. You may even find you forget to add it as you've started the habit of eating well.

"Sleep is like the golden chain that binds our health and body together."

Thomas Dekker

Soothing Pain and Discomfort

Have you ever noticed that when you experience pain it can be unbearable? Yet when someone else has pain, it doesn't register with you how much pain has been a problem for you in the past? And vice versa you don't always get the sympathy you expect. I guess this works in a similar way to childbirth the pain is quickly forgotten or women wouldn't go through it a second time.

Degrees of pain, it all hurts

If you've had your breastbone cut for a cardiac operation, you may feel quite stiff around your shoulders and chest. You'll have been taught how to use a pillow or rolled-up towel to help support your chest. This can help ease any discomfort and help support your chest when you cough.

If you've had coronary artery bypass surgery the wound in your leg or arm may also feel tight and itchy for the first few weeks or months.

Even when stents have been fitted you might experience pain or discomfort. I know I did, it was particularly when I turned on my left side at night.

If you experience headaches and migraines, they can be just as debilitating as major surgery.

If you have fibromyalgia, it is likely that you experience continuous widespread pain. It is often felt throughout all of your body; sometimes it is worse in specific areas such as your back, shoulders or neck.

Change how you feel

Pain is defined as a very unpleasant physical sensation caused by illness or injury. It's a symptom of some physical hurt or disorder; it's a response that protects us from harm and enables our survival.

The body gives a signal to the mind that something's wrong. The mind tells the body what to do about it. Sometimes though the pain system can get confused and work too efficiently or not at all. For example, in emergencies you may feel no pain at all or like amputees that experience phantom limb pain, sometimes it's the body giving the wrong signal.

See pain as a positive thing

Whilst pain makes you miserable and unable to concentrate it is a protective function and messaging system. It helps you learn for example, if you put your hand on a hot cooker ring, your nerves communicate to your brain and your brain then immediately sends a message that your hand hurts. You get this message and straight away pull your hand away from the hot cooker; this then stops your hand from experiencing any more pain. You learn from this experience that something hot will hurt and you avoid putting your hand on a hot cooker ring in the future and avoid further injury.

If you pay attention to your body when you sense pain, you then can take steps to fix what is hurting or causing the pain. Pain also helps us prevent ourselves from injuring a body part even more.

If it didn't hurt to walk on a broken leg, you might keep walking on it and cause more damage.

The same applies after heart surgery and other medical interventions. The pain is there as a reminder to not push yourself and cause more injury. The pain is protecting you, just like pain warns you that something is wrong. So pain can be a good thing, it just makes us feel pretty lousy. It might help for you to remind yourself that your pain, wounds and scars are there because you survived and you have a marvellous story to tell.

What's the solution?

We have over the counter painkillers and we have medication that is prescribed for us by our medical teams and yet sometimes it's just not enough. Even after taking the maximum dose the ache and pain can return, moving hurts, not moving hurts and even if we try ignoring the pain it still hurts.

Not all pain relief has to come from prescribed medicines. There are some natural pain relief methods that can help you cope with and manage pain. It is a case of different strokes for different folks, so read on and try these techniques out. Give them a go, what have you got to lose other than that old pain that you didn't want any way!

So here are some of my top tips to help you self-manage your pain and discomfort.

Remember the positive things about pain and that nothing stays the same. Use any or all of the techniques above but do always contact your doctor if things don't improve or get worse.

Four-square (box) breathing

When you breathe make sure that you're using your tummy, it should rise as you inhale and fall with your exhale. To check this put a hand on your tummy just above your belly button as you breathe.

Take a breath in through your nose slowly and deeply to the count of 4.

- Imagine breathing in peace and calm.
- Hold for the count of 4 as you take a moment.
- Then exhale through your mouth to the count of 4.
- Feel all of the tension and anxiety flow out of you as you let the breath go.
- Hold for the count of 4 as you take another moment.
- Repeat at least 8 times.

Distract yourself

Finding something to distract you is a great way of moving your attention away from the pain. The more and deeper you become involved in an activity, the more you are engaging with life (being in the now) and the less attention you pay to the pain.

Throw yourself 100% into it. It should be enjoyable, something you can become immersed in. It should be interesting, stimulating and hold your complete attention.

- Read a book
- Watch a good film
- Draw or paint
- Play some music
- Do a crossword or Sudoku
- Get a colouring book
- Build a model
- Talk to a friend

Soak in a warm bath

Warmth is a great way to reduce pain, tension and discomfort. It soothes tired, aching muscles and gives you a chance to unwind.

You can add 2-3 cups of Epsom salt; it's believed that magnesium helps to reduce swelling, which is something that helps to combat inflammation.

You might like to add a couple of drops of essential oil but not too much though.
You don't need the bath too hot; just warm enough for you to relax and be comfortable.

Ensure that you are well hydrated as believe it or not you do sweat underwater. If you have difficulty getting in and out of the bath then a hot shower can work wonders too.

Relax into it ...

Pain, tension and discomfort can feel so much worse if you hold yourself uptight. It can be really difficult to relax your body and your mind but it really can have a fantastic effect.

Try holding yourself uptight, shoulders up by your ears, tension in your jaw and hold your tummy muscles tight. Hold your breath in and only breathe shallow breaths. Notice how you feel.

Now exhale all the way out, drop your shoulders down, relax your jaw and let go of your tummy muscles. Breathe slowly and calmly. It's amazing the difference it makes and it only takes a few moments to create the change.

What are you saying?

What is your internal dialogue saying? What are you saying or thinking to yourself?

Begin to notice your thoughts around the pain or discomfort. Are you saying to yourself things like: 'I can't cope', 'it will never stop', 'I'm always in pain' or 'this pain is unbearable'? If so, this is increasing your pain and discomfort, it's adding to a vicious circle of tension and pain. It can make you feel disempowered and a victim.

As you become aware of your thoughts start to use positive phrases such as: 'I've got through this before and I can do it again', 'this will pass as everything changes' or 'I am healthy and whole'.

It might help to keep a pain journal so you can identify your thoughts and make the necessary changes.

Here are a few more ideas of phrases you can use to replace the victim of pain thoughts:

- I find it easy to relax
- My mind is calm at all times
- I easily release all tension in my mind and body
- I am in control of the pain
- Every day I find it easier to control my pain
- Each day I feel less and less pain

Essential oils that help reduce pain

Aromatherapy is the ancient use of aromatic oils for improving your psychological or physical well-being. It is used as a complementary therapy alongside standard pain relief treatments. The oils contain anti-inflammatory, analgesic and relaxing properties. They can be beneficial when inhaled or when used in massage. You can burn incense or candles. Sprinkle a few drops of oil on a cushion/pillow or use a hot stone or oil burner.

Some of the more useful oils that can help with pain relief are:

- Bergamot oil
- Peppermint oil
- Rose oil
- Rosemary oil
- Sandalwood oil

Let it go...
This exercise is rather similar to "Time to unwind" in a previous chapter where I talked about easing anxiety.

You can take a few moments to read through this technique a few times so you can remember and get used to the process. Don't worry if you need to refer back to it, just make sure it is in easy view if you need a reminder.

Alternatively, you can record the instructions on your smartphone or computer and then play them back. Make sure you leave enough time in between to fully follow the instructions in your mind.

Another idea might be that if you know someone that you trust, ask them to read through the instructions so you can follow along. It is just as effective whichever way you choose.

This activity can be done with your eyes open or closed. As you follow through the steps of this activity in your mind use a soothing gentle tone of voice to describe to yourself what you see and hear in your imagination.

- Get comfortable and take a few deep breaths. Take a moment to notice where you feel the pain or discomfort, where is it specifically?
- Describe to yourself what the pain would look, sound like and

feel like. Imagine what shape it is? What colour is it? What size, width, length & depth? Is it smooth or rough? Is it hot, room temperature or cold? Does it vibrate slowly or fast, is it still or moving? Is it loud or quiet? Screechy or bellowing?

- Now imagine moving that representation of that pain out in front of you so it's floating and you can see or hear it. Find out more about the shape/sound. What happens when you move it around, make it bigger or smaller, louder or quieter etc.

- As you visualise the shape/sound/representation you can ask questions such as: What do you really represent for me? What do you need? What message do you have for me? What do I need to know?

- Weird as it might seem pay attention to any answers that come to mind. Any thoughts you have, don't sensor them just notice. You might learn something interesting.

- When you feel ready, ask yourself to confirm that you are ready to let this shape/sound/sensation go.

- If in your thoughts you sense any doubts then ask yourself: What needs to happen for me to let that old shape/sound/representation go now?

- Ask your unconscious mind to make it happen as you breathe in deeply and then out slowly and easily allowing a gentle sigh to be audible.

- Next you can begin to make some changes to that representation of that pain.

- In your imagination start to get creative. What would be a soothing colour? Change the colour of the shape. What is a more comfortable shape? Change the shape and find the one that feels better. Make it smaller or bigger, which size improves the feeling the most? Move it closer or further away, again choose the position that creates the better feeling. Try moving it around if it is static, swinging gently in front of you perhaps. Change the sounds to something melodic, calming and soothing. You can remove any hiss or crackle, turning the volume up or down making the sounds to your liking.

- After you have changed enough elements to feel good, imagine that shape dissolving in front of you there may be evaporating away, maybe jetting off into space, perhaps disappearing as magic dust. It could get larger and larger until it explodes into nothingness. Perhaps smaller and smaller or thinner and thinner until it disappears from sight. Just let it go in any way that seems the most appropriate for you.

- Then take a couple of deeper relaxing breaths, with each exhale allow a gentle sigh to be audible and notice how much better you are feeling already now.

Keep a pain journal

The most important person in any pain management intervention is you! Keep to a routine, don't journal just when you're in pain.

It will help you keep detailed records that can help you to be able to communicate effectively with your doctor, medical practitioner or specialist.

Pain can be so overwhelming, keeping a journal is a great way for you to notice the frequency and degree of pain experienced. It helps identify any triggers such as specific activities, or lack of activity, feelings or emotions. It highlights patterns such as what pain relief has the best result and how much. Which alternative therapies help? If pain is worse after certain foods and what activities are most beneficial? It's best to make between 1-3 entries per day.

Pain Journaling

You are the most important person in any pain management intervention. It will help you keep records that can help you communicate effectively with your doctor and medical teams.

Pain can be overwhelming
Keeping a journal is a great way for you to notice the frequency and the degree of pain that you experience. It helps you identify any triggers such as activities, feelings, emotions or even lack of activity.

It will highlight the patterns such as what pain relief medication and amount has the best result. What of the alternative therapies help? Is the pain worse after certain foods and what activities are most beneficial?

You should ideally make 3 entries per day, morning and noon, again at bedtime. Avoid making an entry at the specific time of a flare-up, keep to a regular routine.

An added benefit to help with pain relief is to express your emotions, too. Write about how you feel, let it out in your journal. It will help you identify the thoughts that keep you stuck in pain. You can then look to change them into more healing and helpful positive thoughts.

Your pain journaling should include
The date and the times of the day.

Along with what activities have you been doing since the last entry? This will help identify something that makes it worse or flares it up.

The number of times you have felt pain? Where did you feel the pain? How long the pain lasted? You might want to capture a description of the pain. You can refer to the symptom word bank at the end of this section.

How intense was the pain, on a scale of 1 to 10? (1 = no pain and 10 = the worst pain imaginable). If you make 3 entries a day, add up the numbers and divide by 3 to give an overall pain rating for the day.

What you have eaten or drank since the last entry? This might highlight if any of these are antagonistic to your level of pain.

To find out what works the best for you it is a good idea to make a note of what medications have you taken and did they give you any relief? What other therapies or techniques have you tried and did they help you? Any actions that gave you relief like standing, lying down or walking around?

How to use your pain journal
In the next section, you will find your pain journal. Use the suggested questions to keep track of your thoughts and feelings throughout the day. It will help you to notice good and bad days. Highlighting trends throughout the day and records what makes a difference to you. It can help change how you feel about that pain.

Set a period of time, perhaps a month, print as many pages as you need. Complete them every day, make no comparison or any judgement until you complete your chosen time period. Use the information you've collected to learn about that discomfort and share it with your doctor, medical practitioner or specialist.

"Once you start approaching your body with curiosity rather than with fear, everything shifts."

Bessel A van der Kolk

General Pain Journal

Today is

Morning pain scale 1-10 & notes	Afternoon pain scale 1-10 & notes	Evening pain scale 1-10 & notes	Add together and divide by 3

Morning

Afternoon

Evening

Thoughts and feelings

DOWNLOAD: www.myheartandmind.co.uk/bookTBGO

Angina Management

Angina is tightness, squeezing, pressure, or pain in the chest. It occurs when an area of the heart muscle receives less blood oxygen than usual.

It's not a disease but a symptom, often a symptom of coronary heart disease (CHD). The symptoms on their own are not life-threatening, but they can be similar to the signs of a heart attack. Always make sure you get medical attention if angina occurs unexpectedly, it doesn't go away, or it doesn't respond to resting or your prescribed medication.

How to use your angina journal

Keeping track of your symptoms, the severity and frequency can be really useful for yourself and your medical team. It helps build a picture over time and may highlight patterns that can help you and your medical team manage it more effectively.

The journal that is provided in the next section and word bank is easy to use. It might be a good idea to check with your doctor to see if there is anything specific, they would like you to capture specifically that would make it more meaningful for them.

Each time you experience symptoms such as pain, discomfort or palpitations fill in a section including the date and the times. This will help with seeing the frequency of occurrences, you may be interested to see it happens more or less than you think it does.

Don't worry about being accurate I don't expect you to be precise or down to the minute. The journal is to support you not create any stress or pressure.

If you think you know what might have triggered your angina write that down.

Common triggers can be things like:

- Eating a large meal
- Emotions
- Exercise
- Going out in cold weather
- No trigger (if there was no trigger that you can think of)

Use a scale of 1 to 10 to rate your pain or discomfort:

1 = mild
3 = somewhat strong
5 = strong
8 = severe
10 = very severe

Describe how the symptoms manifest for you. What did they feel like and where in your body did you experience them? Also, make a note of how long your angina symptoms lasted. The duration of symptoms can depend on the type of angina.

Angina involves any of the following sensations in the chest: usually starting behind the breastbone. The pain often spreads to the neck, jaw, arms, shoulders, throat, back, or teeth. To help you with describing the pain you can find a symptom word at the end of this section. Using these descriptions helps standardise your reporting, however, you may have your own so feel free to use those too.

Make a note of what you did to alleviate the symptoms. It is worth also noting how long it took for the discomfort or pain to subside.

Make sure that you take this journal sheet with you and show it to your doctor at each visit. It will help them see patterns and be able to diagnose and treat you.

If you experience severe or persistent chest pain you must call your emergency services and seek emergency care.

Symptom Word Bank

Sometimes it's hard to find the right words to describe what you are feeling. This word bank is to help you by giving you some suggestions. You may have other words to describe the feelings and situations this list is just for ideas and to get you started.

Pain and discomfort:

A flurry of activity
Burning
Bursting out
Comes & goes
Constant
Crushing
Dull
Fluttering
Fullness
Heaviness
Hot
Intermittent
Lump in chest
Missed beat/s
Palpitations
Piercing
Position (left, right or centre)
Pressure
Sharp
Shoulder blades
Squeezing
Stabbing
Stinging
Storming
Throbbing
Thumping
Tightening
Twisting

Breathing:
Can't catch your breath
Coughing
Hacking
Laboured
Shallow
Shortness of breath
Wheezing

Other symptoms can include:
Chills
Clammy skin
Cramping
Dizziness
Fatigue
Feverish
Heartburn
Indigestion
Lightheaded
Nausea
Sweating
Tired
Weakness

Triggers and onset:
After meals
Bending (over or down)
Carrying certain weights
Climbing stairs (how many)
Exercise (during or after)
Foods (particular type)
Gradual
Overwhelming
Reaching out (stretching)
Sitting
Standing
Stooping
Sudden movement
Time of day
Time of night
Walking
Watching Television
Weather (hot, cold, damp, windy)

"It is not the delicate neurotic person who is prone to angina, but the robust, the vigorous in mind and body, the keen and ambitious man, the indicator of whose engines is always at full speed ahead."

William Osler

Angina Journal

Date & time	What do you think triggered the angina?	Rate from 1 to 10	Describe the feelings of discomfort, where in your body and how long did your symptoms last?	What did you do to ease your symptoms and discomfort?
18/11/2020 at 3pm	For example: Cold weather, after or during exercise, taking the stairs, after a big meal.	1 = mild to 10 = severe	For example: Stabbing pain, middle of chest for 10 minutes. You can refer to your symptom word bank checker on the previous page.	For example: I stopped and rested. Used GTN spray.

DOWNLOAD: www.myheartandmind.co.uk/bookTBGO

Ready to Stop Smoking?

I was a smoker for over 30 years. Although in those years I half half-heartedly tried to give up I never particularly wanted to quit until I had my heart attack. I suppose like many others I thought it would never happen to me. I didn't know about the genetic factors that I couldn't change. But I did know about the risk that smoking caused and contributed to my event.

Smoking is responsible for 19% of all deaths from coronary heart disease (British Heart Foundation 2000). I am now smoke-free; I do think about it from time to time but I wouldn't say I miss it now – it's just something I used to do.

This chapter is to help you with ideas and suggestions that you can use to prepare to quit smoking or vaping that will increase your success. Preparation is the third stage of change, getting ready to become a non-smoker once and for all.
The first two stages are **pre-contemplation** and **contemplation.** You can read about these in more detail in by blog www.myheartandmind.co.uk/blog. I have written a number of posts about stopping smoking or vaping, just add these words to the search bar.

It is now time to consider the best options and strategies to help you become a non-smoker.

This stage is like the foundations of a house. It will hold you up if things get tough. It gives you a solid plan to refer to. It will motivate you to keep moving forward. It is a reminder of your choices and the benefits of quitting smoking.

At this stage, it is likely that part of you wants to quit smoking, but part of you doesn't. Maybe you're worried about withdrawal, or afraid that you'll fail. Put those thoughts aside, for now, don't believe all the myths.

Focus on your why, the reason you want to quit and it will give you the drive to succeed.

**You CAN quit smoking
with a little help and organisation.**

A great way to get ready to quit smoking is to create a quit plan. The following ideas will help you create your own personalised toolkit. Read through them and tick the ones that feel that they will be helpful. By doing this you will be able to identify any challenges you'll face as you quit and how you can overcome them.

You can combine any number of them and create your very own quit kit to help you stop smoking once and for all. Your kit will keep you focused, confident and inspired.

These activities will increase your chances of quitting smoking forever.

Learn from the past
You might have tried to quit smoking before and not managed it. Don't let that put you off. Look back at the things your experience

has taught you, the lessons learned. Think about what you can put in place to avoid what tripped you up before. You're really going to do it this time.

Make your plan to quit smoking

Choose when you will quit smoking. Make a promise, set a date, mark it on the calendar and stick to it. Remember that there will never be the right time. Just decide, come hell or high water, that this is the date you will stop.

How are you going to quit?

Research all your options. There are many methods to help you quit smoking. Make a list and work out the pros and cons of each. It may be that you decide on a combination or just one way. Whatever it is, it will be the right thing for you right now. Decide and just do it!

Decide to stick to the 'not a drag' rule

It will really help. Whenever you notice yourself struggling with wanting a smoke, say to yourself, 'I will not have even a single drag' repeat over and over again. Stick with this until the cravings pass.

Think ahead

Give some thought to the future. There will be occasions and times where it might be more difficult - a party, for instance, get ready with a plan. Work out what your actions will be and any escape routes in advance. Don't stand with other smokers.

Consider your diet

Is your after-dinner cigarette your favourite? A US study revealed that some foods, including meat, make cigarettes more satisfying. Others, including cheese, fruit and vegetables, make smoking taste terrible. Plan to swap your usual steak or burger for a veggie meal instead; it's not forever just for a short while.

Change up your routines

You may want to change your routine after mealtimes. How about getting up and doing the dishes straight away, it will be a distraction. What else can you change, how about your morning routines and habits?

Vice versa

Start to break your habit. If you have a regular smoking place, then smoke somewhere else. If you smoke at the back door, start only smoking at the front door. Then the reverse, turn your usual smoking place into a non-smoking area. Make it fag free and do something else there, like read the paper or a magazine.

Clean your car and wash your clothes

If you smoked in your car, get it cleaned inside and out. Get rid of all reminders of smoking or vaping. Check the door pockets and the glove box. Wash your clothes too, get rid of the smell of smoke from any soft furnishings as well.

Change your drink

If you connect smoking or vaping with certain drinks you may need to make a short-term change. Research has found that fizzy pop, alcohol, cola, tea and coffee all make having a smoke taste better. Plan to drink more water and if you are a tea drinker, swap to coffee or fruit tea instead.

Alcohol and you

When you are socialising and alcohol is available, it can be difficult. Some people find that simply changing their drink makes a difference. For example, try switching from wine or beer to vodka and orange for a change. This simple switch can affect your desire to reach for a cigarette. What are you going to change?

Identify when you crave cigarettes

A craving can last five minutes. Make a list of 5 minute strategies for the situations where you think you are likely to crave.

For example, if you are at a party or at the pub you could leave the party for a minute, have a dance, or go to the toilet. At other times it might be to chew gum or have a glass of water. Stop what you are doing and do something/go somewhere different.

Become aware of your smoking

Practice being more conscious of smoking. Start to use your other hand to hold your cigarette when smoking. Yes, it will feel strange and awkward, a bit like trying to write with your other hand. It will make you more conscious of your smoking.

Check your habits?

Do you have strong links to having a cigarette while you are drinking tea, coffee or wine? If so, change it up so that you only smoke before or after the drink – not with it. This will begin loosening the link and help break the habit. What changes do you need to make in your life to break the connection to the old smoking habit?

When do you reach for a smoke?

(Take a moment to tick all that apply)

- ☐ After a meal
- ☐ After breakfast
- ☐ Before going in to work
- ☐ Before I go to bed
- ☐ During elevenses
- ☐ In conversation with others
- ☐ To help me relax
- ☐ When I finish a job or task
- ☐ When I first wake up
- ☐ When I have a lunch break
- ☐ When I need to concentrate
- ☐ When I want to feel confident
- ☐ When I'm alone
- ☐ When I'm at work
- ☐ When I'm bored
- ☐ When I'm nervous
- ☐ When I'm feeling stressed
- ☐ When I'm in the car

- ☐ When I'm on the phone
- ☐ When socialising with friends
- ☐ With my morning cuppa
- ☐ Other ....
- ☐ Other..................
- ☐ Other.................

Watch yourself smoking or vaping

When you smoke become aware of the cigarette in your hand. Notice it burning, the red tip, the smoke and chemicals burning off it. Watch as you put the cigarette/vape to your lips, notice the feeling of it against your lips. As you inhale notice the feeling of it going inside you. The taste in your mouth and the smell of the chemicals as they enter your body.

Look at the smoke/vapour as you exhale leaving your body and emptying your lungs. Be present as you smoke.

Wanted vs enjoyed that fag

Use a scale of 1-10 (1 = not a lot and 10= ever so much). Choose a number that expresses how much you wanted that cigarette before you have it. Make a note. Then after you smoked it choose a number that demonstrates how much you enjoyed it. You might be interested to see how the two don't match up.

Self-belief

Believe in you, you do have the ability to make this change to become a non-smoker. Take some time to make a list and remind yourself of all the other things you have achieved in your life.

Particularly think about the things that have been difficult. List the exams you've passed, the new jobs or promotion, learning to drive, really quite complicated. There will be lots of things if you think about it, start the list and add to it as time goes on. You can do it.

What's in it for you

Prepare a list or be creative with drawings to help you focus on what becoming a non-smoker will do for you and your family. Think of all the things that when you have kicked the habit and stopped smoking will be different. You will be fitter, healthier and better off financially. You will have more energy and be free from the inconvenience of smoking or vaping.

Create a vision board

A little bit woo-woo! But heck give it go. Cut out pictures of all the things that you can do once you have quit smoking. Perhaps you'll be able to afford a holiday of a lifetime. Maybe you can walk upstairs without getting out of breath. You'll smell fresh and clean; your hands and fingers will not be stained with nicotine. The new clothes you can afford, the places you can go that you avoid because you can't smoke. All that extra time you gain, what will you do with that?

Ask for help

You'll be surprised at how many people have quit themselves and are happy to support you. Remember everyone wants you to succeed – they are always there to help and support you. Especially if they used to be smokers themselves.

Enlist some stop smoking support

Search the Appstore or Microsoft store for the latest and most recommended Smoking Apps for your phone. You can use them to keep a tally of the time since you quit and your success?

Use Google to search for Quit smoking forums and websites. If you're in the UK, you can visit the NHS smoke-free website. Get in touch with a local hypnotherapist. Contact your doctor's surgery.

Get ready to be accountable

Once your date is booked and set tell people you are stopping smoking. This gives you a focus and helps others to prepare to support you too.

Get moving

Plan some exercise, even a five-minute walk or stretch, it will distract you from cravings. It will help your brain produce feel-good chemicals that will help reduce cravings.

Meet up with your non-smoking friends

Prepare by arranging some dates in your diary to spend some time with your friends that don't smoke. Plan some activities that will fill your time so that you have less time to dwell.

Watch other smokers and vapers

Start 'people watching', pay attention to all the smokers around you. When you look at them, don't envy them. Examine their behaviour and think about what they're doing as a bit strange. Lighting a small white tube, filled with poison then they breathe in the chemical-laden smoke. In the cold & rain. Trapped by the habit.

Talk to your smoking friends

You may need to make some changes. It is better to explain and plan ahead of quitting. Talk to the people that you smoke with and tell them that for a while you will not be joining them at smoke time. Avoid going outside with them for at least 2 weeks although a month would be better.

Your list of reasons to quit

This will remind you why you made the decision to give up. Write a list of all the reasons that you want to quit so you can refer to it later. If it's hard start to think about the excuses to smoke and reverse them. This will then be ready for you to read when you need support and encouragement.

Calculate how much money you spend

You literally watch it go up in smoke. Go on grab a calculator. Let's do the math. Write these figures down so you can use them to inspire you to continue if you feel like it's getting tough.
How much do you smoke per day? ______________

How much does it cost per day? ______________

Multiply by 7, that's how much per week? ______________

Multiply by 4, per month? ______________

Multiply by 12, that how much per year? ______________

How many years you have been smoking? ______________

Then calculate your lifetime spend? _____ x _____ = _____

Portable hobby
Start to consider what activities you can use as a distraction. Are then any electronic games you can play on your phone or tablet? Maybe you knit or do needlework, you could take a project with you.

How about listening to a podcast or audiobook. You could learn another language. Carry a colouring book. Start writing songs or poetry. What can you use as a distraction, what can you do to fill the gaps where you would have smoked? These will also occupy your mind and body if you do have a craving.

Turning back time
Once you've set your quit date add it to your diary, calendar or notebook. Then include the following benefits so you can see how well you are doing. You'll be aware of the benefits of stopping even when you can't see or feel them.

- After 20 minutes - Pulse rate returns to normal.

- After 8 hours - Nicotine and carbon monoxide levels in your blood reduce by more than half and oxygen levels return to normal.

- After 48 hours - Carbon monoxide will be eliminated from the body. Lungs start to clear out mucus and other smoking debris. There is no nicotine in the body. Your ability to taste and smell is improved.

- After 72 hours - Breathing becomes easier. Bronchial tubes begin to relax and energy levels increase.

- After 2-12 weeks - Your circulation improves.

- After 3-9 months - Coughs, wheezing and breathing problems improve as lung function increases by up to 10%.

- After 1 year - The risk of heart disease is about half compared with a person who is still smoking.

Create a streak
Get yourself a wall calendar or a method of marking off days in your diary. Your intention will be to put a big tick on each day that you don't smoke. You'll see the running streak and it will motivate you not to have a missed day. A visual reminder of how well you are doing.

Get essential
A 2013 study published in the Journal of Alternative and Complementary Medicine found that when nicotine users inhaled the scent of black pepper oil, their cravings were reduced. They reported a slight burning sensation in the throat, which is similar to the sensation they had when smoking.

Put a drop of the oil on a cotton wool ball (keep it in a small glass jar) and then inhale it when a craving becomes noticeable.

Sleep

Some people experience insomnia for a couple of nights after they quit smoking. Get a plan together of how you will manage this should you be affected. There is some evidence to suggest that herbal remedies can be effective for insomnia. The most commonly used ones to treat insomnia are valerian, passionflower, hops, lavender, lemon balm and Jamaican dogwood.

Relaxation

Get some lavender scented candles or incense. Lavender has been useful for treating anxiety, insomnia and restlessness. It is physically and emotionally calming, relaxing and balancing. For an immediate calming effect rub a drop or two of lavender oil into your cupped hands. Inhale deeply drawing the scent into your amygdala (the emotional warehouse) to calm your mind and body.

Reward, reward, reward

Decide in advance that, once you have stopped smoking, you will give yourself a reward. You will absolutely deserve it. What is going to be your mile-stone date and how will you celebrate it? Make sure you have that one thing to look forward to.

It's the little things too

It's not just about that big mile-stone; make sure you also map out in your diary some other successes. How will you reward yourself? For instance, how about celebrating your one-day target, your one-week achievement, your two-week goal and your one-month triumph?

Time on your hands

It can be amazing how much time you gain when you've stopped smoking. Start to plan how you are going to adjust your life to fill the void that being a non-smoker will leave? For example, you may want to consider getting up later so you don't have time to walk leisurely to work or have time to have a cigarette in the morning.

The next step to stopping

The great news is that it doesn't matter how long you have smoked or how many cigarettes you have smoked it's not too late. If you quit now, your body will begin to heal and it will be there for you even after many years of smoking.

You are now ready for the next step to take action and become a non-smoker.

Get support

If you want to join a group specifically for people that are living with a heart health diagnosis that want to quit smoking or vaping, come over to Facebook and join my free group called Smoking Hearts! **www.facebook.com/groups/smokinghearts**

If you are a smoker or vaper that wants to quit and has had a heart attack, cardiac event, or lives with a heart disease diagnosis, this group is for you.

You may have tried to quit but haven't quite managed it yet. Maybe you did quit originally but have gone back to smoking. Perhaps you want to quit vaping and be free from the addiction to nicotine.

Primarily this group is a safe and nurturing place for you to support each other. I have created it so you can discuss smoking without feeling judged or feeling like you've failed. It's a place where you can share ideas, tips, experiences and ask for support. You can speak freely and openly, ask for help, accountability, and what worked for others. It is not for encouraging smoking.

There is a lot of pressure to quit smoking when you have heart health issues. Not least of all this pressure comes from yourself.

You want to live a life of freedom from the habit, feel more in control of your life, have a healthier heart, and enjoy living life happy. You are fed up with the thoughts that cross your mind, that you are actually killing yourself or shortening your time with loved ones.

Maybe that's too strong but have you had those thoughts?
In this community, we will help each other to quit and support each other as we do. Word of warning in my experience people that are still smoking do not want others to quit as it makes them feel lousy that they can't do it themselves. And that is okay, we need to be honest with ourselves and face this together.

I am passionate about this because I had a heart attack in 2016. I was a smoker since the age of 14 and was 52 when I had my MI. I quit from the moment that I was blue lighted to the Cath Lab and thought I would never smoke again. However, I did! It was harder to quit the second time, mainly because the shock element was missing and I wasn't in the hospital for a week, I guess.
It was from the hearty groups on Facebook that I realised there were others like me that had continued or restarted smoking or vaping that desperately wanted to stop.

I will share what I know with you in the group as I have worked 1:1 with many clients to help them quit smoking.

The first thing for you to remember is that you CAN think, feel and behave differently.

"I have not failed.
I've just found 10,000 ways that won't work."

Thomas Edison

Cardiac Terminology Guide

Are you confused by the cardiac terminology and abbreviations that are associated with your heart health? I know I certainly was; this cheat sheet will help.

To be able to have meaningful conversations with your doctor, cardiologist or medical specialist you need to speak the same language.

This Cardiac Terminology Guide cuts through the confusion and will help you to understand some of the common terms that are used by your specialists. You will feel more in control and know what is meant in meetings and in documents that are about you.

It's a glossary of commonly used heart and vascular-related medical terms. Explanations of words used to discuss or describe heart illnesses.

Everything you need to know to help you understand your cardiac health and what your cardiac team and your doctor are talking about so that you feel more in control of your life.

A wave: Atrial wave

ABPM: Ambulatory blood pressure measurement

ACE: Angiotensin-converting enzyme

ACEI: Angiotensin-converting enzyme inhibitor

ACS: Acute coronary syndromes

ADH: Antidiuretic hormone

Aerobic exercise: Activity which requires continuous rhythmic muscle contraction of the legs and/or arms.

AF: Atrial fibrillation

AICD: Automatic implantable cardioverter defibrillator

ALT: Alanine aminotransferase

Anaemia: A deficiency in the oxygen-carrying material of the blood.

ANCA: Antinuclear cytoplasmic antibody

Aneurysm: A pathological blood-filled dilatation of a blood vessel. Bulging of the wall of a vein, artery, or heart due to weakening by disease, injury, or birth defect.

Angina Pectoris: Also called stable angina. Angina pectoris is the medical term for chest pain or discomfort due to coronary heart disease. It occurs when the heart muscle doesn't get as much blood as it needs. This results in pain in the chest and often in the left arm and shoulder.

Angina: Pain due to an inadequate supply of oxygen to the heart muscle. The term angina is now used almost exclusively to denote angina pectoris, the medical term for chest pain or discomfort that is most often due to coronary heart disease. Stable angina refers to episodes of chest discomfort that are usually predictable and which occur on exertion or under mental or emotional stress. Unstable angina refers to episodes of chest discomfort that are unpredictable and usually occur while at rest.

Angiogram: An angiogram is a type of X-ray used to examine blood vessels. Blood vessels don't show up clearly on ordinary X-rays, so a special dye is injected into the area being examined. The dye highlights the blood vessels as it moves through them. The medical name for this is a catheter angiogram.

Angioplasty: A procedure with a balloon-tipped catheter to enlarge a narrowing in a coronary artery. This is also known as percutaneous transluminal coronary angioplasty (PCTA).

Anticoagulant: Medicine which delays clotting of the blood. If given when a blood vessel is blocked by a clot, it tends to prevent new clots from forming or the existing clot from enlarging, but does not dissolve an existing clot.

Antihypertensive: 1. Counteracting high blood pressure. 2. An agent that reduces high blood pressure.

Antithrombotic: An agent used to prevent or interfere with the formation of a thrombus (a blood clot in a blood vessel or within the heart.

Aorta: Largest artery in the body. It carries blood from the heart's left ventricle and distributes it throughout the body.

Aortic: Related to the aorta, which is the major vessel that carries oxygenated blood from the heart to the body. Sometimes this term is used to denote the aortic valve, which is the valve that prevents back-flow of blood from the aorta into the left ventricle. (For example, 'aortic stenosis.')

AR: Aortic regurgitation

ARB: Angiotensin receptor blocker

Arrhythmia: A condition in which the heart beats with an irregular or abnormal rhythm. Too fast, too slow or erratic.

Arteriosclerosis: Condition in which the walls of the arteries thicken and lose their elasticity, thus decreasing blood flow through them. May be due to a build-up of fibrous tissue, lipids, or minerals. Also called hardening of the arteries and usually occurs naturally with aging.

Artery: The vessel that carries blood away from the heart. Arteries generally carry oxygenated blood. In mammals, the exception is the pulmonary artery, which carries deoxygenated blood to the lungs.

AS: Aortic stenosis

ASD: Atrial septal defect

AST: Aspartate aminotransferase

Atrial Fibrillation: Atrial fibrillation is an irregular and often rapid heart rate that occurs when the two upper chambers of your heart experience chaotic electrical signals. The result is a fast and irregular heart rhythm.

Atrium: Is the two upper chambers of the heart. The chamber of the heart that collects blood returning from the rest of the body. In all vertebrates but fish, there are two atria, left and right. The right atrium collects deoxygenated blood from the body and passes it to the right ventricle. The left atrium collects oxygenated blood from the lungs and passes it to the left ventricle.

AV: Atrioventricular

AVN: Atrioventricular node

AVNRT: Atrioventricular nodal re-entrant tachycardia

AVR: Aortic valve replacement

BHF: British heart foundation

Blood clot: A semi-solidified mass of blood, either in or out of the body.

Blood pressure: Pressure of the blood on the walls of the arteries, produced primarily by contraction of the heart muscle. Its measurement is recorded as two numbers: the first (systolic pressure) is measured after the heart contracts and is highest; the second (diastolic pressure) is measured before the heart contracts and is lowest.

Body mass index (BMI): Index for relating a person's body weight to his or her height. The body mass index (BMI) is a person's weight in kilograms (kg) divided by the person's height in meters (m) squared.

BP: Blood pressure

BPM: Beats per minute

Bradycardia: Abnormally slow heart rate. Generally, any rate under 60 beats per minute.

CABG: Coronary artery bypass grafting

CAD: Coronary artery disease

Cardiac arrest: Occurs when the heart stops beating and the circulation of blood ceases.

Cardiac catheterization: Test done by putting a long, narrow, flexible tube into a blood vessel and guiding it into the heart to measure the mechanics of blood flow and to determine the position and size of structural defects.

Cardiomyopathy: Disease of the heart muscle that reduces the ability of the heart to pump enough blood. This is the general term for diseases of the heart muscle (myocardium). The most common of these diseases is the dilated cardiomyopathy in which the disease weakens the heart muscle and causes left ventricular dilation leading to increased diastolic pressure and volume.

Cardiopulmonary resuscitation (**CPR**): Emergency measure used by one or two people to try to revive a person whose heart and breathing have stopped.

Cardiovascular: Pertaining to the heart, blood and blood vessels.

Cardioversion: Use of low voltage electric shock to stop an abnormally fast heart rhythm through paddles placed on the chest surface.

Carotid endarterectomy: A surgical procedure designed to clean out material blocking the carotid artery, a major artery in the neck that supplies blood to the brain. The aim of the procedure is to restore normal blood flow to the brain, thereby preventing a stroke.

Catheter: Thin, flexible tube which can be guided into a body organ.

Catheterisation Lab: A catheterisation laboratory, commonly referred to as a Cath lab, is an examination room in a hospital or clinic with diagnostic imaging equipment used to visualise the arteries of the heart and the chambers of the heart and treat any stenosis or abnormality found.

Cerebrovascular: Pertaining to the blood vessels of the cerebrum, or brain.

CFM: Colour-flow mapping

CHD: Coronary heart disease

CHF: Chronic heart failure

"Where lies the line between sorcery and science? It is only a matter of terminology, my friend."

Alan Dean Foster

Cholesterol: Also known as total cholesterol. A fatlike substance that is a building block of the outer layer of cells (cell membranes). It is essential to the formation of bile acids, cell membranes, vitamin D and certain hormones. Cholesterol is not dissolved in the blood, but is transported in the bloodstream as water-soluble molecules known as lipoproteins. The lipoproteins are characterized by their density: high density lipoprotein (HDL) and low-density lipoprotein (LDL).

CK-MB: Creatine kinase myocardial band fraction

Claudication: Cramping of the muscles (typically the calf muscles) with exercise, produced by inadequate blood flow.

CNS: Central nervous system

Congestive heart failure: Inability of the heart to pump blood with normal efficiency. When this happens, the heart is unable to supply enough blood to the body's other organs such as brain, liver and kidneys. Symptoms can include shortness of breath, pooling of fluid in the legs and feet, swelling and enlargement of the heart.

Coronary arteries: Arteries arising from the base of the aorta which carry blood to the heart muscle.

Coronary artery bypass graft (CABG): Surgery done to bypass narrowed or obstructed areas to improve blood flow. A surgical procedure whereby a new route is created around plaque within a coronary artery, using part of a vein as a graft. The procedure permits increased flow to deliver oxygen and nutrients to the heart muscle.

Coronary heart disease (CHD): Condition caused by narrowing of the coronary arteries resulting in decreased blood supply to the heart (ischemia). It begins when hard cholesterol substances (plaques) are deposited within a coronary artery. The plaques in the coronary arteries can rupture cause the formation of a tiny clot, which can obstruct the flow of blood to the heart muscle, producing symptoms and signs of CHD that may include chest (angina), heart attack or sudden death due to a fatal disturbance of the heart rhythm. Also known as coronary artery disease (CAD).

Coronary occlusion: Obstruction in a coronary artery which interrupts flow of blood to the heart muscle. Also called a heart attack.

Coronary: Relating to the heart, or to one of the two arteries that originate in the aorta and supply blood directly to heart tissue.

CPR: Cardiopulmonary resuscitation

CRP: C-reactive protein

Cryoablation: It is a minimally invasive procedure in which the specialist uses a thin flexible tube, known as a balloon catheter, to locate and freeze this heart tissue. Cryoablation is an appropriate treatment for atrial fibrillation when medications and other AF treatments do not restore the heart to a normal rhythm.

CT: Computed tomography

CW: Continuous wave

Cx: Circumflex artery

CXR: Chest x-ray

Cyanosis: A condition in which a person's skin is discoloured to a bluish hue because of inadequate oxygenation of the blood.

DC: Direct current

DCM: Dilated cardiomyopathy

Defibrillation: Use of high voltage electric shock to stop an abnormally fast heart rhythm through paddles placed on the chest surface (external) or around the heart (internal).

Diabetes mellitus: Disease characterized by high levels of glucose in the blood caused by a failure of the pancreas to produce enough insulin or by ineffective use of insulin in the body.

Diastole: Normal period of relaxation and dilatation of the heart cavities.

Diastolic pressure: The minimum blood pressure, measured before the heart contracts. Usually, the second number recorded in a blood pressure reading.

Dilatation: The condition of being abnormally dilated or enlarged.

Diuretics: Medicines which increase the flow of urine. Often used to treat conditions involving excess body fluid, such as hypertension and congestive heart failure.

Dyspnoea: Difficulty or shortness of breathing. Laboured breath.

E wave: Early wave

ECG: Electrocardiogram

Echocardiogram: Test in which pulses of sound are sent into the body and the echoes returning from the surfaces of the heart produce images that are recorded.

ED: Erectile dysfunction

EDV: End diastolic volume

EEL: External elastic lamina

EF: Ejection fraction

Ejection fraction (EF): is a measurement, expressed as a percentage, of how much blood the left ventricle pumps out with each contraction. An ejection fraction of 60 percent means that 60 percent of the total amount of blood in the left ventricle is pushed out with each heartbeat.

Electrocardiogram (EKG or ECG): Graphic record of the electrical activity of the heart. A recording of the electrical activity of the heart. It is a simple, non-invasive procedure whereby electrodes are placed on the skin of the chest and to a machine that, when turned on, measures electrical activity all over around the heart. An example of its clinical use is in the initial stage of a heart attack, which is usually made by a combination of clinical symptoms and characteristic EKG changes; the EKG can detect areas of muscle (muscle deprived of oxygen) and/or dead tissue in the heart.

Electrophysiology study (EP study): Test done to evaluate the heart's electrical conduction system by inserting small catheters into the heart and reproducing symptoms and rhythm disturbances in a controlled setting.

Embolism: Blocking of a blood vessel by a blood clot or other substance carried in the blood stream.

ESD: End systolic dimension

ESR: Erythrocyte sedimentation rate

GFR: Glomerular filtration rate

GP: Glycoprotein

Haemorrhage: Profuse loss of blood or bleeding.

Haemorrhagic stroke: Rupture of a blood vessel in or near the brain. This type of stroke accounts for 20% of all strokes that occur. There are two types of haemorrhagic stroke: haemorrhage, which occurs when a blood vessel on the surface of the brain ruptures and bleeds into the space between the brain and skull; and haemorrhage, which occurs when a blood vessel bleeds into the cerebrum, the main portion of the brain.

HCM: Hypertrophic cardiomyopathy

HDL: High-density lipoprotein

Heart attack: See also myocardial infarction. Death of the heart muscle due to the loss of blood supply, usually caused by a complete blockage of a coronary artery, one of the arteries that supplies to the heart muscle. Death of the heart muscle, in turn, causes chest pain and electrical instability of the heart muscle tissue. Also known as infarction (MI).

Heart block: Condition which results in a block or a slowing of the electrical impulses which travel through the heart.

Heart Lung Machine: A machine that does the work both of the heart and of the lungs: pumping and oxygenating blood. Blood returning to the heart is diverted through a heart-lung machine before being returned to arterial circulation.

Heart rate: Number of times the heart beats in one minute.

High blood pressure: A repeatedly elevated blood pressure exceeding 140 over 90 mmHg - a systolic pressure above 140 with a diastolic pressure above 90. Also known as hypertension.

High density lipoprotein (HDL): A fat-like substance that transports cholesterol from the tissues of the body to the liver so it can be excreted in the bile. HDL is the so-called 'good'; the higher the HDL cholesterol level, the lower the risk of coronary heart disease (CHD).

HIT: Heparin-induced thrombocytopenia

HMG-coa: Hydroxymethylglutaryl coenzyme A

Hypercholesterolemia: Excess of cholesterol in the blood.

Hyperlipidaemia: Excess of fats or lipids in the blood.

Hypertension: High blood pressure. A condition in which a person's blood pressure is abnormally high. For normal adults, the pressure should be less than 130 mmHg systolic and less than 85 mmHg diastolic. Pressures above 140/90 indicate a mild form of hypertension; above 180/110 is considered severe.

Hypotension: Low blood pressure.

IABP: Intra-aortic balloon pump

ICH: Intracranial haemorrhage

ICS: Intercostal space

ICU: Intensive Care Unit

IE: Infective endocarditis

IEL: Internal elastic lamina

IM: Intramuscular

Infarct: Area of tissue which is damaged or dies because of a blocked blood supply.

INR: International normalized ratio

Insufficiency: Describes a condition in which a valve is not able to prevent back-flow of blood. The resulting back-flow is termed a regurgitation.

Intensivist: An intensivist is a board-certified physician who provides special care for critically ill patients. Also known as a critical care physician.

Irregular rhythm: Heartbeat that is unpredictable and without pattern.

Ischemia: Temporary deficiency of blood and oxygen in a portion of the body, often caused by a blockage in the blood vessel supplying that part.

IV: Intravenous

IVC: Inferior vena cava

IVDA: Intravenous drug abuser

JVP: Jugular venous pressure

LA: Left atrium

LAD: Left anterior descending artery

LBBB: Left bundle branch block

LDH: Lactate dehydrogenase

LDL: Low-density lipoprotein

LIMA: Left internal mammary artery

Lipid: Term for fat or fat-like substance found in the blood, such as cholesterol.

LLSE: Left lower sternal edge

Low density lipoprotein (LDL): A fat-like substance that transports cholesterol from the liver to the tissues of the body. LDL is the so-called 'bad' cholesterol; elevated LDL levels are with increased risk of coronary heart disease (CHD).

LP(a): Lipoprotein little a

LP: Lipoprotein

LPL: Lipoprotein lipase

LV: Left ventricle

LVESD: Left ventricular end-systolic dimension

LVH: Left ventricular hypertrophy

Mammary artery: The internal thoracic artery (ITA), previously commonly known as the internal mammary artery (a name still common among surgeons), is an artery that supplies the anterior chest wall and the breasts.

MET: Metabolic unit

METs (metabolic equivalent): Units of measurement of the energy required to perform a physical activity. One MET is the energy used by your body while sitting quietly in a comfortable chair.

MI: Myocardial infarction

Mitral valve: Valve that separates the left atrium and the left ventricle and prevents back-flow from the ventricle to the atrium. Derived from 'miter,' which it resembles. (A miter is a tall, pointed hat with peaks in front and back which is worn by a bishop.)

MR: Mitral regurgitation

MRA: Magnetic resonance angiography

MRI: Magnetic resonance imaging

MS: Mitral stenosis

MV: Mitral valve

MVA: Mitral valve area

MVP: Mitral valve prolapse

Myocardial infarction (MI): The medical term for heart attack. It refers to changes that occur in the heart muscle (myocardium) due to the sudden deprivation of circulating blood. The change is necrosis (death) of myocardial tissue.

Nuclear Heart Scan: Also known as Nuclear Stress Test, Radionuclide Scan. A nuclear heart scan is an imaging test that uses special cameras and a radioactive substance called a tracer to create pictures of your heart. The tracer is injected into your blood and travels to your heart. This imaging test can detect if blood is not flowing to parts of the heart and can diagnose coronary heart disease. It also can check for damaged or dead heart muscle tissue, possibly from a previous heart attack and assess how well your heart pumps blood to your body.

NYHA: New York Heart Association

Oedema: Swelling that occurs when the body tissue contains more fluid than normal.

Pacemaker: Small mass of specialized cells in the right atrium of the heart which initiates the electrical impulses that produce contractions of the heart. An implanted pacemaker is an electrical device which can control the beating of the heart by creating one or more rhythmic electrical impulses.

Palpitations: Sensation of fluttering of the heart.

PCI: Percutaneous coronary intervention

PDA: Persistent ductus arteriosus

Percutaneous transluminal coronary angioplasty. Procedure of stretching open a coronary artery with a balloon catheter to improve blood flow to the heart muscle.

Perfusionist: A healthcare professional who operates the cardiopulmonary bypass machine (heart–lung machine) during cardiac surgery and other surgeries that require cardiopulmonary bypass to manage the patient's physiological status.

Pericardium: Closed sac around the heart.

PET: Positron emission tomography

Phlebitis: Inflammation of any vein, often in the leg.

Plaque: Deposit of fat or other substances in the lining of the arterial walls.

Platelet Inhibitor: An agent/therapy which prevents or interferes with the formation of blood clots in blood vessels.

Polyunsaturated fat: A fat containing polyunsaturated (a term used to denote more than one unsaturated bond - that is, more than one place where hydrogen can be added to the molecule) fatty acids, molecules derived from animal and vegetable fats and oils. Unlike saturated fats, polyunsaturated fats are considered beneficial in that they lower cholesterol.

Prolapse: Floppy valve, associated with regurgitation.

PTCA: Abbreviation for percutaneous transluminal coronary angioplasty. Procedure of stretching open a coronary artery with a balloon catheter to improve blood flow to the heart muscle.

PTCA: Percutaneous transluminal coronary angioplasty

PTSD: Post Traumatic Stress Disorder

Pulmonary artery: Artery that transports blood needing oxygen from the heart to the lungs.

Pulmonary: Relating to the lungs. Sometimes this term is used to denote the pulmonary valve, which is the valve that prevents back-flow of blood from the pulmonary artery into the right ventricle. (For example, pulmonary regurgitation).

PW: Pulsed wave

Qtc: Corrected QT interval

RA: Right atrium

RAD: Right axis deviation

RBBB: Right bundle branch block

RCA: Right coronary artery

Regurgitation: Back-flow of blood through an insufficient valve. (For example, mitral valve regurgitation).

RF Ablation: Catheter ablation is a procedure that uses radiofrequency (RF) energy (similar to microwave heat) to destroy a small area of heart tissue that is causing rapid and irregular heartbeats. Destroying this tissue helps restore your heart's regular rhythm. The procedure is also called radiofrequency ablation.

RIMA: Right internal mammary artery

Risk factor: Characteristic that has been shown to increase one's chances for developing a disease or making a disease worse.

RV: Right ventricle

RVH: Right ventricular hypertrophy

SA: Sinoatrial

SAN: Sinoatrial node

Saphenous Vein: Large vein in the leg which can be grafted onto the heart in coronary bypass surgery to provide adequate coronary circulation.

SCA: Sudden cardiac arrest

SCAD: Spontaneous coronary artery dissection

Sinus Rhythm: Normal heart rhythm.

SLE: Systemic lupus erythematosus

SND: Sinus node dysfunction

SPECT: Single photon emission computed tomography

SR: Sinus rhythm

Stenosis: Constriction of a passage. Used typically when there is a narrowing of a valve opening (for example, mitral valve stenosis) or of a blood vessel.

Stent: A stainless steel device that helps hold any artery open. It is placed by a balloon catheter inflated in the artery.

Stress test: A stress test is an electrocardiogram recorded before, during and after exercise. It shows how the heart muscle reacts to the increased heart rates and blood pressures included by exercise.

Stress: Physical, mental or behavioural response of the body to demands made on it by a stressor. This response is based on individual interpretation. Forces from the outside world impinging on the individual. Stress releases powerful neurochemicals and hormones that prepare the individual for action. If none is taken, the stress response can lead to health problems such as depression, high blood pressure or heart attack.

Stroke: The sudden death of some brain cells due to a lack of oxygen when the blood flow to the brain is impaired by blockage (ischemic stroke) or when a blood vessel breaks and bleeds into the brain (haemorrhagic stroke).

A medical emergency, stroke is also called a cerebrovascular accident (CVA).

Stroke symptoms depend on the area of brain affected.

The most common symptom is weakness or paralysis of one side of the body, with partial or complete loss of voluntary movement or in a leg or arm; other symptoms can include speech problems, confusion, weak facial muscles, numbness or tingling.

A stroke involving the base of brain can affect balance, vision, swallowing and breathing and may even cause unconsciousness.

SVC: Superior vena cava

SVT: Supraventricular tachycardia

Syncope: A brief loss of consciousness caused by temporary lack of oxygenated blood.

Systole: Period of contraction of the heart during which blood is ejected from the ventricles.

Systolic pressure: The maximum blood pressure, measured after the heart contracts. Usually, the first number recorded in a blood pressure reading.

Tachycardia: Fast heart rate. Generally, any rate above 100 beats per minute.

Tc: Technetium

TEE: Transoesophageal echocardiography

TGA: Transposition of the great arteries

Thrombosis: Formation of a blood clot (thrombus) inside a cavity of the heart or blood vessel.

TIMI: Thrombosis in Myocardial Infarction

TM: Tunica media

TNF: Tumour necrosis factor

TPA: Tissue plasminogen activator

TR: Tricuspid regurgitation

Trans fat: An unhealthy substance, also known as trans fatty acid, made through the chemical process of hydrogenation of oils. Hydrogenation solidifies liquid oils and the shelf life and the flavour stability of oils and foods that contain them. Trans fats drive up levels of LDL ('bad') cholesterol, which increases risk of heart attack and stroke.

Transient ischemic attack (TIA): A neurological event with the signs and symptoms of a stroke, but which go away within a short period of time. Also known as a mini-stroke, a TIA is due to a lack of adequate blood and oxygen (ischemia) to the brain. TIAs typically last from 2 to 30 minutes and can produce problems with vision, weakness or trouble speaking. If not treated, a TIA carries a high risk of having a major stroke in the near future; people who have a TIA have a % risk of stroke or other serious complication within 90 days.

Tricuspid valve: Valve that separates the right atrium and the right ventricle and prevents back-flow from the ventricle to the atrium. It is composed of three leaf-like parts.

Triglyceride: The major form of fat. A triglyceride consists of three molecules of fatty acid combined with a molecule of the alcohol glycerol. Triglycerides serve as the many types of lipids (fats). Triglycerides come from foods and are also produced by the body. Triglyceride levels do not provide clinically information about the risk of coronary heart disease (CHD) beyond that provided by levels of HDL and LDL cholesterol.

Vascular: Pertaining to blood vessels.

Vein: One of the blood vessels which returns blood from various parts of the body towards the heart. Usually carries deoxygenated blood.

Ventricle: One of the two main pumping chambers of the heart. The left ventricle pumps blood to the body, while the right ventricle pumps blood to the lungs.

VLDL: Very low-density lipoprotein

VO2: Max maximum rate of oxygen consumption

VSD: Ventricular septal defect

VT: Ventricular tachycardia

WPW: Wolff–Parkinson–White syndrome

Wrapping Up, it's time to say 'Until Next Time'

It's been an honour being welcomed into your life and I've really enjoyed being able to share some of my ideas with you. Just like life, change is an ongoing process. With this in mind, your change to any new situations has to be too, it's fluid and an ongoing process.

Make the most of every moment because life is a journey and not a destination.

Pay attention to the techniques that worked best for you and continue using them. Did you have some kind of measurable outcome in mind? Where are you now? What do you want to happen next?

None of the activities I have shared with you are revolutionary. None of them will create change by themselves but when combined, the results are life-changing. How you think, feel and behave are changing and it's all been down to you. You've got stuck in, you've been determined and curious about how life can be different.

All the techniques that we have covered certainly aren't exhaustive. If you've loved the results, you've already achieved you can increase them even more. If you've had a great time and it's made a real difference please recommend this book to your family, friends and colleagues.

You can and will transform as you have done so many times before.

Wishing you love, luck and laughter.

Inspiring you to survive and thrive emotionally after a cardiac event or when living with heart disease! If in any doubt always check it out and seek medical advice.

About the Author

Sallie Crawley has over 17 years' experience as a coach and therapist. She is a certified Life Coach and ILM Executive Coach and Mentor. She is also certified as a Master Practitioner of Neuro Linguistic Programming and trained as a Clinical Hypnotherapist.

Since overcoming breast cancer and surviving a heart attack, she specialises in helping people who have had a heart attack learn to live life and love life again. She helps with anxiety, panic, sleeplessness, creating the mind-set to make exercise & dietary changes, relaxation, smoking cessation and confidence.

As a North Londoner, her career was originally in the print and communications industry. Spending some 16 years she gained experience working in commercial, report and accounts and food labelling printing companies. She managed teams in admin, production and sales.

After a year out to be a full-time mum and a move to a small village, Sallie had a career change. In 2002 she joined the RSPB (conservation charity) and supported volunteering throughout the UK for 17 years. As the HQ Volunteering Operations Team Manager, she is inspired and proud of the contribution that the Charity's 12,000+ volunteers make to the cause.

Sallie also proudly volunteers as a Trustee of a local charity, the Hunts Cancer Community Network (HCCN). Empowering patients to take control of their diagnosis and take an active part in managing their health. By providing services in the areas of education, wellbeing, exercise and nutrition. HCCN is helping to transform cancer care in the Huntingdonshire Community.

She lives in Cambridgeshire, UK with her daughter, their dog, two cats and a fish called Lonely.

Other Books by Sallie

Cognitive Cardio - Puzzles for a Healthy Heart & Mind. Pass the time, stimulate your brain, and learn more about your heart health during cardiac recovery through crosswords and puzzles.

UK https://amzn.to/3Lt3p7v
US www.amazon.com
AU www.amazon.com.au
CA www.amazon.ca

Beyond The Beat - Your guide for before and after heart surgery or a heart attack for emotional resilience. Taking back your life with actionable steps.

UK https://amzn.to/4bpZwei
US www.amazon.com
AU www.amazon.com.au
CA www.amazon.ca

Staying in Touch

Read more My Heart & Mind articles
www.myheartandmind.co.uk/blog

Visit the My Heart & Mind website
www.myheartandmind.co.uk

Listen to the My Heart & Mind podcast
www.myheartandmind.co.uk/podcast

Join the My Heart & Mind community
www.facebook.com/groups/myheartandmindcommunity

Quit smoking with me
www.facebook.com/groups/smokinghearts

Get in touch by email
sallie@myheartandmind.co.uk.

"It's okay to have therapy. It's okay to take medication. You deserve to heal, be happy and be healthy."

Sallie Crawley

Printed in Great Britain
by Amazon

51903251R00112